REAL LEADERSHIP

WAKEN TO WISDOM

SUSAN ROBERTSON

ISBN: 978-1-950336-01-2

TABLE OF CONTENTS

THE JOURNEY

*"The journey of a thousand miles begins
with a single step."*
—*Tao Te Ching*, **Laozi**

There is a single quality that separates truly great leaders from the average, and that is the ability to be real.

REAL leadership is forged in the heart and soul. Without heart and soul, we lead from fear and habit. We play out programmed behaviors and beliefs rather than what is deeply true from within. When leaders are REAL, they lead transformational cultures and engagement, and corporate performance is no longer an issue.

In today's world of hacking, subterfuge, lying, stealing, and cheating, being REAL is not merely a good strategy; it is the best strategy for leading organizations.

To be REAL means waking up. Waking up to the inner truth of who we are and what drives us. It requires an honest look in the mirror to acknowledge that we are not perfect. Waking up means we are willing to transform ourselves from fear-based mindsets and behaviors to become a better person than who we are today. Becoming a REAL leader requires authenticity, humility, caring, transparency, and discernment. Most importantly, REAL leaders are egoless and serve the greater good.

Becoming REAL means remembering that we are the master programmer of how we act and respond to anything that happens to us. Being REAL means changing our reactive mindsets and creating a proactive mindset. It means we transcend the limitations of a programmed past and become who we really are beyond our programming. We change who we think we are and become who we truly are. Ask yourself, *If I created programs of personality, habits, and emotional reactions, who is the me that created those programs to begin with?*

Most of us mold ourselves from the events of our past. We have predispositions that we are born with, and we develop habits over time. These habits, or programmed beliefs and behaviors, develop as a result of significant emotional events and life-defining moments. We become creatures of habit, acting on our internal programming, forgetting that we are the programmer.

> *"Don't be pushed around by the fears in your mind.*
> *Be led by the dreams in your heart"*
> —Roy T. Bennett, *The Light in the Heart*

We are the programmers of our thoughts, beliefs, emotional reactions, and habits. With the discovery of quantum physics and epigenetics, we now know that our thoughts, beliefs, and emotional reactions can biologically program our brain, creating neural networks that hold patterns in place. These neural networks become the programmed foundation of our habits.

What we "think" of as being ourselves can be part of our programmed selves. We say things like, "I'm just emotional" or, "I am blunt; people have to get over it." We now understand that these types of self-definitions are just that—definitions we created. If we have a pattern of behavior that is no longer useful, we can change. Period.

> *"The latest research supports the notion that we have the natural ability to change the brain and body by thought alone... Because you can make thought more real than anything else, you can change who you are from brain cell to gene, given the right understanding".*
> —**Dr. Joe Dispenza,** *Breaking the Habit of Being the Yourself: How to Lose Your Mind and Create a New One.*

Sometimes, we forget that we are the creators and programmers of our self-definition. If we forget that we created the programs, beliefs, and thoughts in our own minds, it becomes much more difficult to change our habits and programs. If we aren't the creators of our beliefs and our perspectives, then we are the victims of our circumstances. When we live from that mindset, we find it difficult to battle fear, pain, hurt, and the unknown, and we lose the opportunity to create and transcend our situation. We lose the ability to go beyond our limited thoughts and behaviors and become reactive rather than proactive. This has a significant impact on those we lead, and this ultimately affects organizational results.

Life-defining moments and self-definition

As I will discuss later in the book, our personal history and the events of our lives have a huge impact on the beliefs we develop, the defensive structures we create, the personality characteristics we adopt, and the way we behave.

I have great memories of growing up in San Diego from the age of four to seven. I loved the school I went to. We had great neighbors. The church where I received my First Holy Communion is still, to this day, the most beautiful church in my memory. The playground behind the church is surrounded by steep cliffs, and I can remember playing four corners (a ball game) there with my friends. I remember our entire school standing in the playground saying the pledge of allegiance every day, playing outside on sunny days, and the beaches of Mission Bay. These amazing and happy memories are stored in the neural networks of my brain, and in the emotional muscle memory of my body.

In 1968, my mother divorced, and my grandmother moved in to help my mother raise four girls. Then, in early 1969, my grandmother died of cancer. It was a very difficult time in our lives. My mother was a young, single mother raising four girls on her own, paying for Catholic school tuition, and trying to have her own life. Despite these difficulties, the memories of playing in our yard on sunny days, with the ice cream man driving through the neighborhood outweigh even those difficult times.

My mother went through her changes and got back on her feet to start over. She fell in love, we moved to Cleveland, she remarried, and nine months later, my youngest sister was born. Now, there were five girls in our family. While my memories from San Diego are full of sunshine and laughter, my early memories after moving to Cleveland, in contrast, are dark, sad, and painful. After our move to Cleveland, our family faced a lot of emotional trauma, sexual abuse, and poverty.

Just like my positive memories, these extremely difficult memories are encoded and stored in the neural networks of my brain and in the emotional muscle memory of my body. I mention this because these types of events, both positive and negative, impact the way each of us programs our beliefs. We create many of our beliefs based on our life-defining experiences. It is also true that we are given beliefs that we adopt. For example, I was "born" Catholic. I didn't have a choice about being Catholic. My mother felt Catholicism would provide a strong education and moral foundation for us, plus, according to my mother's work on our family tree, our family has been Catholic for centuries. Later, I chose to be Catholic.

Beliefs are the foundation for how we think, act and behave. Depending on the kinds of life experiences you've had, you will have a myriad of positive and negative beliefs that form the foundation of your thought and behavioral patterns. When we experience traumatic times, such as poverty and abuse, we create survival beliefs. As a result of my difficult times, I made a vow that things like poverty and abuse would never happen to me again. Unbeknownst to me at the time, I made a vow to transcend my current situation and to create a new life for myself. This vow was deeply ingrained and became a driver of my life. Somehow, I learned a key behavior that is one of the cornerstones of this book—I learned and taught myself how to transcend the present situation and create a new life.

REAL Leadership

Becoming a REAL leader—even a transcendent leader—is a journey of thousands of steps. And yet, it begins with a single step. Consider Martin Luther King, Jr. Not only was he a transformational leader; he was an example who provided the roadmap for self-transformation. Through his sermons, he implored us to treat each other with kindness and compassion. He had a dream and created a movement of equality and justice. His dream consumed him. The reality of his time, and even today, was racial inequality. But he took the steps to transform himself and share that dream with the rest us of. As a result of his honesty, authenticity, integrity, ego-lessness, and selflessness, with passion for the greater good of humanity, his dream still guides many people today.

Martin Luther King, Jr. realized that if he wanted to change the world, he needed to have a dream and turn it into a purpose. That purpose allowed him to transcend the reality of his time to build and create something new. He had to believe in possibility and change.

This book is about how to build a conscious culture by becoming a REAL leader. It is about creating your own dream as an individual and leader to build conscious cultures that can change the way we do business today. Throughout this book, I will be using REAL leadership, transcendent leadership, and conscious leadership interchangeably. Being REAL means taking the journey of personal transformation to become more aware and conscious and to move beyond the known to courageously move into the unknown.

We are taught that the sole purpose of business is to maximize shareholder value. I dispute this premise. Yes, businesses need to be profitable to survive. Without profitability, the business dies. Profitable businesses help communities and the economy. But conscious businesses with conscious cultures include focusing on sustainability, not profitability alone. Conscious and sustainable organizations are those companies that include making a difference for the community at large and being purpose driven as primary values. This can only be driven by REAL leaders.

Conscious businesses create organizations that improve the world community. Many organizations are now focused on creating a sustainable future. Take Microsoft, for example. They have social responsibility programs that help refugees, create programs of education, provide drinkable water, and grow food in impoverished communities. The organization also researches to help prevent the damage of climate change, and this is, in part, because Microsoft sees themselves as part of a global community. That is not to say that Microsoft is perfect and that they have a perfect culture. There are many things they do that are imperfect. At the same time, what Microsoft is trying to do is make a difference while creating a profitable business. What many conscious businesses are learning is that maximizing shareholder value includes social responsibility programs. This leads to a purpose-driven culture that can make a difference.

Conscious businesses with conscious cultures require conscious, REAL leadership. It means changing the message that *profitability* is the most important goal to a balanced view of organizational success. The new definition of healthy and successful companies needs to include a balanced focus of *profitability*, *giving back,* and committing to *meaningful work*. The first step is to change ourselves as leaders, to wake-up and become conscious leaders.

> *"If you want a new outcome, you will have to break the habit of being yourself, and reinvent a new self."*
>
> —**Dr. Joe Dispenza,** *Breaking the Habit of Being Yourself: How to Lose Your Mind and Create a New One*

The Millennial generation wants to work for organizations where they can both make a living and make a life. They want to work for organizations that are making a difference. They want to know that what they do makes a difference. This gives them purpose. Many business leaders ask me, "How do I deal with these Millennials?" I usually laugh because most business leaders I work with are part of the Boomer generation. I often reply, "We raised Millennials. We taught them to 'do what they love, and the money will follow.' We taught them to find meaning and purpose in their lives and that their work should reflect that. Millennials are our children who are demanding change, and they won't settle for less."

Profitable, conscious cultures mean that leadership demonstrates the change they want to see.

"To change a culture, the leaders have to change the messages people receive about what they must do to fit in. When people understand that there are new requirements for belonging, they adjust their behavior accordingly....A small change in a senior manager's behavior can send a big message."

—**Fred Kofman,** *Conscious Business: How to Build Value through Values.*

Chapter 1 of this book is about the leadership journey, waking up and discovering what it means to become a REAL, conscious leader. Facing your inner reality is the first step and is key to unlocking your full potential as a person and a leader of others. I have found that the leaders who wake up and break free from unconscious and fear-driven behaviors tend to become truly great leaders because they are REAL, human, authentic, touchable, fallible, compassionate, and selfless.

Becoming a REAL leader starts with examining how we behave. Many of us have strong, positive intentions and believe in noble causes. But when pressured, many of us don't have enough resilience to push back and say, "Some of these goals are unrealistic." So, we compromise ourselves, our values, and our integrity. We try hard to achieve unrealistic goals, and we end up feeling overwhelmed, tired, and stressed.

To be truly successful, as a leader and in life, becoming REAL means you have internal integrity because your beliefs, intentions, and behaviors are internally aligned.

Chapter 2 focuses on how we derail and get off-track from waking up and becoming REAL. As I shared before, many of us are driven by unconscious fears, habits, and bias. Self-awareness and direct honesty with ourselves allow us to recognize our off-purpose behaviors so that we can make a conscious choice to change. If we are not conscious and self-aware, we live by habit.

To become a transcendent leader—and before we begin the leadership journey of becoming REAL—we must find the True North of our inner compass. Our True North is our inner compass that drives our behavior. This is our deeper Self. However, we may not follow our inner compass due to fear. If we don't address our internal fear, we lose our internal compass. Unfortunately, there is a lot of fear inside organizations. As leaders, if we don't face our individual fears, these become collective fears and part of the culture. Eventually, these collective fears not only block us individually from reaching the pinnacle of our capabilities, but they also adversely impact organizational culture and engagement. This is when businesses begin to fail due to fear-driven cultures. Organizations lose their ability to be agile and innovative when fear drives the culture. However, if leaders face and change the fear inside of themselves, they start to transform the organization.

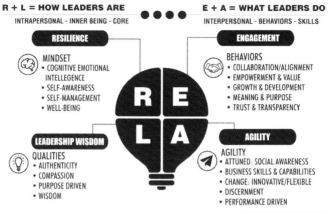

| R + L = HOW LEADERS ARE | E + A = WHAT LEADERS DO |
| INTRAPERSONAL - INNER BEING - CORE | INTERPERSONAL - BEHAVIORS - SKILLS |

RESILIENCE

MINDSET
• COGNITIVE EMOTIONAL INTELLEGENCE
• SELF-AWARENESS
• SELF-MANAGEMENT
• WELL-BEING

ENGAGEMENT

BEHAVIORS
• COLLABORATION/ALIGNMENT
• EMPOWERMENT & VALUE
• GROWTH & DEVELOPMENT
• MEANING & PURPOSE
• TRUST & TRANSPARENCY

LEADERSHIP WISDOM

QUALITIES
• AUTHENTICITY
• COMPASSION
• PURPOSE DRIVEN
• WISDOM

AGILITY

AGILITY
• ATTUNED: SOCIAL AWARENESS
• BUSINESS SKILLS & CAPABILITIES
• CHANGE: INNOVATIVE/FLEXIBLE
• DISCERNMENT
• PERFORMANCE DRIVEN

© SUSAN ROBERTSON: REAL LEADERSHIP: WAKEN TO WISDOM

REAL leadership is a way of leading. It is both a leadership style and personality type. Chapters 3, 4, 5, and 6 focus on the elements of REAL Leadership, how to become conscious and wake up, and develop wisdom. When we transcend our limitations, we become a transcendent leader who can lead cultural transformation. But first, let's break down exactly what REAL means.

The *R* stands for Resilience, and the *L* stands for Leadership Wisdom. The R and L have to do with the internal nature of a person. I call this the intrapersonal dimension of leadership and self-development. Resilience is all about self-awareness, self-management, cognitive and emotional intelligence, and well-being. Resilience refers to the beliefs we hold, the habits we've developed, and how well we manage stress.

Leadership Wisdom refers to authenticity, compassion, insight, discernment, selflessness, purpose-driven behavior, and making decisions for the greater good over the advancement of the self. We can only develop wisdom as we learn to let go of our defenses and act out of choice rather than defensiveness.

The E and the A represent the interpersonal dynamic of the REAL Leadership model. These aspects represent the behavioral dynamic that occurs between people. How well do we engage, empower, listen, challenge, develop people, and drive positive behaviors organizationally? How comfortable are we with change, innovation, risk-taking, and outside-the-box thinking? Are we agile and adaptive or do we continually look to maintain the status quo?

REAL leadership starts with resilience. To become resilient, we need to develop the skills of consciousness and awareness. Resilience is vital because our ability to be resilient impacts how exactly we engage, influence, and impact others. Without strong resilience, we become more close-minded and less agile.

Becoming more self-aware, learning from our mistakes, and having the willingness to move past our own ego-centric behavior allows us to develop leadership wisdom. REAL leadership is about developing deep inner wisdom to drive inner peace, success, and personal happiness. By becoming a REAL leader, your organization can improve its bottom-line success.

This book will show you where you and your organization need to be—and how to get there. You will discover what it means to be "REAL," to be honest, transparent, compassionate, authentic, tough, caring, discerning, wise, intelligent, and direct. REAL leadership ultimately leads to deep inner wisdom. Wisdom comes with age, experience, and—most importantly—a willingness to be deeply honest, admitting flaws and mistakes, and having the willingness, courage, and strength to internally learn, grow, and transform.

Chapter 7 discusses how you can become a transcendent leader. Transcendence means to become more expansive, to become something that's greater than the reality of today. Being a REAL and transcendent leader requires moving beyond the confines of our current reality to create new, more powerful solutions to the problems and issues we face in today's complex business requirements.

Chapter 8 moves into how to take the next step and make an impact as a leader by developing a REAL, conscious, and transcendent culture.

> *"Many fears are born of fatigue and loneliness.*
> *Strive to be happy."*
>
> —*Desiderata,* **Author Unknown**

The journey begins

The nucleus of this book concerns helping you become a leader who knows how to inspire others, pull together a community toward a common goal, and drive results. All leaders need these traits to become good leaders. So, what is the difference between a good leader and a REAL Leader who can lead transformation and even transcendent organizations? You will find the answer to this question later in the book.

This book is about "becoming." REAL leaders know how to face themselves in the mirror and be directly honest with themselves. REAL leaders objectively recognize their strengths and weaknesses, changing from the inside-out to become inspiring and selfless leaders. REAL leaders learn to cultivate wisdom by letting go of their ego, and they listen to their inner guidance, their True North.

Welcome to the journey. I hope this book will help you cultivate your ambitions in becoming a REAL leader.

Chapter 1

Being REAL

*"Leadership development is a lifetime journey,
not a quick trip."*
—John Maxwell

Within all leaders is the power to be self-aware, conscious, wise, and transcendent--a REAL leader. This means transcending personal limitations, biases, judgments, habits, and stereotypes. A REAL leader is someone who, by their nature and practice, is wise, humble, transparent, authentic, ego-less, compassionate, and selfless.

The REAL and *transcendent* leader has the vision and intent to make the world a better place. *Summum bonum* is a Latin expression that means, "for the highest good." Conscious leaders live and breathe *Summum bonum*. They focus on what is best for all concerned: shareholders, the organization, co-workers, their family, and the community at large. They go beyond the present day, solving the problems at hand and meeting objectives while focusing on and creating the dream of tomorrow. REAL leaders create movements that people want to be a part of and follow. This requires the skill of transcendence.

A good leader is someone who has a powerful influence on others. They know how to get things done. They drive the vision and mission forward. They create strategies, plans, and objectives. REAL Leaders do the same and more. They have lasting influence because they show deep respect and genuine care for others. Because of these qualities, they create followership. They are the servant to those they lead. REAL leaders create a passion and a glue that hold teams together to create high performance.

To become a transcendent leader, we must first go through a personal journey of deep inner transformation. This takes courage to face and move beyond our limitations. It is a journey of pain, but with it is the reward of discovery, realization, and joy. Becoming REAL is not an easy process. It is a journey that can take a lifetime. Becoming REAL is a great adventure of personal self-discovery to make a difference in the world. One of my favorite books is *The Velveteen Rabbit*. In the book, the Skin Horse counsels the Rabbit on what it means to become REAL.

> *"Real isn't how you are made,' said the Skin Horse. 'It's a thing that happens to you. When a child loves you for a long, long time, not just to play with, but REALLY loves you, then you become Real.'*
>
> *'Does it hurt?' asked the Rabbit.*
>
> *'Sometimes,' said the Skin Horse, for he was always truthful. 'When you are real you don't mind being hurt.'*

*'Does it happen all at once, like being wound up,' he
asked, 'or bit by bit?'*

*'It doesn't happen all at once,' said the Skin Horse.
'You become. It takes a long time. That's why it doesn't
happen often to people who break easily, or have sharp
edges, or who have to be carefully kept. Generally, by
the time you are Real, most of your hair has been loved
off, and your eyes drop out and you get loose in the
joints and very shabby. But these things don't matter at
all, because once you are Real you can't be ugly, except
to people who don't understand."*

—**Margery Williams Bianco**, *The Velveteen Rabbit*

Becoming REAL is a journey of the heart and soul. Like
the Rabbit, the journey starts with curiosity and a deep
desire to become REAL. To become REAL, we must
transcend our limitations of who we think we are and
continually challenge our smaller, more limited self-
definition.

According to an article published in *Forbes*,
"transcendent leaders rise above or go beyond the limits of
the small 'self,' moving into the REAL 'Self.' They triumph
over the limitations of what might be considered acceptable
or possible. The small 'self' operates from a limiting
exclusive focus on scarcity. Transcendent leadership
operates from the REAL 'Self,' precipitating an unbounded,
inclusive focus on abundance."

REAL transcendent leadership is about expansion. It's
about creativity, innovation, and inspiration. When leaders
move beyond limitations, they move into the space of

limitlessness, where true inspiration can occur. In spiritual doctrine, this space of limitlessness and expansion is often called Universal Consciousness. When we stay small and limited in our thinking, believing, and behaving, it is much more difficult to dream and inspire movements that can create fundamental change and innovation.

Learning how to transcend mental and emotional programs and move into a fulfilling state of inspiration and expansion starts with quieting the mind and coming to the still point within. When we practice quieting the mind and obtain inner silence, we are no longer bound by our limitations. Becoming a REAL leader means we are transcending our personal limitations and leading others to do the same.

Becoming conscious of our beliefs, needs, and drivers

We all have beliefs, needs, and underlying drivers that operate in the background of our subconscious, like the hard drive of a computer. Using our RAM (Random Access Memory)—our conscious mind—we can reflect on how we feel and think at any given moment. We generally know if we feel hot or cold, if we are comfortable or uncomfortable, or whether we are tired or energized.

But when it comes to our mental, emotional, and behavioral responses, we are generally not conscious of the drivers behind them.

Psychologist Abraham Maslow, in his 1943 paper, *A Theory of Human Motivation*, developed a five-part pyramid prioritizing human needs, known today as Maslow's

Hierarchy of Needs. This model has a lot to teach us. On the foundational level are our basic physiological needs, such as rest, food, and warmth. The peak of the pyramid is self-actualization, which is, evidently, difficult to attain if you are struggling to have a roof over your head.

The one area that has not been studied enough is Maslow's 6th need, which is transcendence. *"Self-transcendence is, at its core, about transcending (or rising above) the self and relating to that which is greater than the self. In simpler terms, it is the realization that you are one small part of a greater whole and acting accordingly."* (Maslow. What is self-transcendence? *Positive Psychology*). As a leader, transcendence means we must rise above our personal needs and fears and lead from a place of *Summum bonum*.

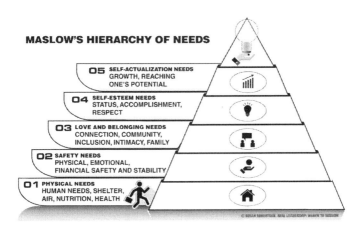

To become a fully realized and transcendent leader, we must balance the needs of ourselves, others, and our organization. We need to acquire the ability to rise above all the needs of all of our various stakeholders to see a broader picture. This requires strategic skills, discernment, and future vision.

> *"A transcendent leader is a strategic leader who leads within and amongst the levels of self, others, and organization. Leadership of self includes the responsibility of being self-aware and proactive in developing personal strengths. Leadership of others involves the mechanisms of interpersonal influence a leader has upon followers. Leadership of organization comprises the alignment of three interrelated areas: environment, strategy, and organization. Propositions are presented regarding the relationship between leadership of the various levels and firm performance."*
>
> —**Crossan, Vera, and Nanjad,** *Transcendent Leadership: Strategic Leadership in Dynamic Environments*

Going off the rails

Two years ago, I was walking through the Atlanta airport on my way to Mexico City. I was meeting with several clients who wanted support with transforming their culture. One of my clients is the CEO of an organization that needed to be turned around. His organization struggled with inventory issues, logistics, different parts of the organization not communicating when needed, and old-legacy ways of doing things.

Many of the leaders inside the company had been there for 25 years or more and were set in their ways. At one point, this organization was the best in the business, but it had begun to lose market share a few years earlier. Even though they were making headway on improving their inventory system, tracking the movement of merchandise, and improving online purchasing, and they weren't growing. Despite having the best brands and the best facilities, the market share of this organization continued to decline. They weren't attracting new customers, and old customers were starting to leave. Upon carrying out market research, they noticed their brand was old and "stodgy." Younger clients didn't want to be associated with them and opted for the newer competitors in the market. The CEO felt it was time to look at the culture to discover what was happening.

What the CEO learned is that many of the managers had neither the desire to improve customer relationships nor did they feel it was important to integrate with other departments. Sales had no idea of the inventory. The stores had no clue what was happening at other stores. Purchasing would make their decisions on getting the best deal rather than what was needed for the market. Without communication between the various parts of the business, time, money, and market share was being lost.

For many years, teamwork and inter-departmental communication were not rewarded. In fact, they were actively discouraged. After conducting a baseline cultural and leadership assessment, it turned out that three of the main business units and the Presidents of each company actively withheld information and avoided each other. The culture study revealed that the Presidents of these three main business units were highly controlling. Instead of collaborating, they developed silos, each of them thinking they were right to do so. But this was just the tip of the iceberg! When we investigated further down the organization, the general feel of the culture was that you could get away with anything and that no one cared about your performance levels or if you made a mistake. This organization needed to transform. But the organization, to transform itself, had to identify the behaviors of the leadership team that needed to change. This organization could only remake itself if the leaders remade themselves and how they interacted and led the organization. They needed to transcend their individual habits and biases, their individual need to be right, and, as a team, rise above themselves. In other words, this leadership team needed to wake up and transform individually and collectively. They needed to get real with each other and face the tough issues that prevented them from working together as a team.

As in *The Velveteen Rabbit*, sometimes, becoming REAL and transcending our current situation can be a painful experience. It's not easy, especially when we like our habits and our comfort zone. However, pain often leads to rebirth, and this rebirth can yield powerful results.

Waking up

This executive team needed to wake up to the fact that *they* were the problem. While there were processing issues, inventory issues, and logistical issues, the leadership team did not address the issues because they were not talking to each other. They were not educating, training, or empowering their people. They were not collaborating and aligning.

"True leaders don't create more followers;
they create more leaders."

—Tom Peters

Think about a sports team. Each player must play their role and play it well. Everyone has a set of skills. A team is highly successful when they utilize each other's strengths and help cover for the weaknesses. Additionally, for sports teams to win, they must collaborate and communicate. In the previous example, this corporate team needed to change its ways and act more like a successful sports team.

In this example, the team went to the "team collaboration" gym. The leaders assessed their own individual effectiveness as leaders and their collective impact leading the organization. Two of the three main leaders were controlling, aggressive, and domineering. The third leader—the head of procurement—didn't like conflict and laid low as a consequence.

When the CEO brought people together to figure out ways to work better together to solve the issues the organization faced, everyone would play nice in front of him. The CEO knew this was happening, but he too was a conflict-avoider and didn't hold his team to creating and working toward an aligned strategy.

Jerry, one of the leaders, was especially controlling, domineering, and aggressive. He needed to take a long, hard look in the mirror. He was the President of the largest business unit and did not play well with others. Yet, his business depended on inventory and logistics. He recognized he held grudges against people. He realized he was full of fear. He thought he needed to control everything. He stayed focused and "siloed" rather than playing team ball with the other two key leaders. This hurt his results. He would blame, deny, and defend his position instead of reaching out to solve issues collaboratively. This is how the journey began for the entire team. It started with Jerry taking responsibility and accountability for his leadership behaviors. This allowed the other two leaders to accept responsibility for their role in the issue. For Jerry and the team, this was the beginning of the REAL leadership journey.

> *"Forces beyond your control can take away everything*
> *you possess except one thing, your freedom to choose how*
> *you will respond to the situation."*
> —**Victor Frankl,** *Man's Search for Meaning.*

Becoming a REAL Leader starts with the desire for transcendence. In order for Jerry to change, he had to want to change. Transcendence is the desire and the need to make a significant impact in this world. Jerry wanted and desired to be an exceptional leader. He wanted to transcend his limitations.

The transcendent leadership journey starts with building inner resilience through vulnerability, compassion, authenticity, and well-being. Physical well-being is important because if we aren't rested, we are more prone to react emotionally. Digging a little deeper, Jerry struggled with stress. Because he had to do it all and control it all, he was continually worried, barking orders in the hopes of making his organization successful. Jerry needed to let go and be more open. But letting go of control requires vulnerability, and transcendent leaders realize that it takes inner strength and courage to be vulnerable, reachable, and touchable. Transcendent leadership is a journey of peeling back the onion of personal history and emotional habit patterns, reaching beyond limitations and fears, and creating a future that has deep meaning and purpose.

> *"I suppose you are real?" said the Rabbit. And then he wished he had not said it, for he thought the Skin Horse might be sensitive.*
> *But the Skin Horse only smiled.*

> *"The Boy's Uncle made me Real," he said. "That was a great many years ago; but once you are Real you can't become unreal again. It lasts for always."*
> —**Margery Williams Bianco**, *The Velveteen Rabbit*

Peeling back the onion: Jerry's story

Jerry was a key player in this organization. He led the largest business. He had the largest number of stores and employees, along with territory. His business unit generated the most revenue and, consequently, had the largest impact on margin and profitability. Jerry was highly intelligent, persistent, and very, very stubborn. There was only one way to do things, *the right way*, which equated to *Jerry's way*. Unfortunately, in his business, Jerry had become a bit of a dinosaur. While he understood the business of fitness, he had not changed with the times. He had not kept up with the evolving trends of consumers and what they really wanted in brick-and-mortar access. He had two main leadership issues: lack of resilience and low agility. Although he was dedicated to high performance, when he got stressed, the more controlling, domineering, and aggressive he became.

Jerry needed to become more flexible and agile to ideas. He didn't listen to what others had to offer, so he missed a lot of important information. Agility is the capability to be flexible and innovate, to see beyond the current box and create a new box. Agility is the ability to discern when to stay with the status quo and when to take a risk and move beyond the known.

We all have biases and blind spots. Often, we don't recognize our biases until we are in trouble. Trouble can come in the form of negative feedback, not getting the job promotion, or even being fired. Part of becoming REAL is consciously learning to transcend our blind spots and biases by actively seeking them out. What Jerry failed to realize is that the success he was looking for would have been much easier to reach had he been open to other people's ideas rather than just his own.

> *"Groups with diverse backgrounds and skills are usually far superior to any single expert in evaluating solutions. Each person's strengths, weaknesses, and biases average out into opinions that are surprisingly accurate."*
>
> —**Scott Thorpe,** *How to Think Like Einstein: Simple Ways to Break the Rules and Discover Your Hidden Genius*

Jerry needed to peel back the layers of the onion to find out what drove him to lead the way he did. It meant looking at life-defining experiences from childhood onwards and learning what type of defensive structures had manifested in him, which caused him to derail as a leader.

Due to his low resilience, the aggressive, domineering, and micro-management side of himself came out easily, demonstrating that his engagement and influencing skills needed improvement. His "command and control" approach made many of his peers not want to work with him. This made his job more difficult. Rather than having a high-performing team, his direct reports waited to be told what to do. The he controlled everything, the more work he had to do. This created a vicious cycle for Jerry. He didn't realize how much his leadership behavior adversely impacted his effectiveness. He thought the direct reports were lazy. He was scared of failing. He felt his entire work reputation was on the line. Out of fear, he controlled every decision. The more controlling he got, the more his business' market share declined. Jerry's leadership style led to a whole company of disempowered and uninspired people.

As his results continued to decline, he could no longer lie to himself. There is a saying that goes, "if everything around me is a problem, and I can't see why, the common denominator is likely me." The more Jerry struggled to "push" his team into driving results, the more elusive the goal became. He slowly began to recognize that the more he tried to control things, the more likely he was going to fail. This kick-started Jerry to start peeling back the layers of the onion and look at his leadership impact.

*"It's only after you've stepped outside your comfort zone
that you begin to change, grow, and transform."*

—Roy T. Bennett

I love to cook and experiment with recipes. I like to see how different flavors relate to each other. As cooks, we know the trinity of savory foods is garlic, onions, and celery. When I experiment with a savory dish and need to chop onions, I know I will probably cry. As we peel back our own layers of the onion, we have to cry before we hit the sweet center.

For Jerry, peeling back the layers meant that he needed to unpack his deeper motives and intentions. One of the deeper insights Jerry realized is that he held a grudge against his boss. He explained that a few years ago, his boss said something in public he disagreed with and was still angry about it. Instead of confronting his boss and talking it out, he became belligerent and rebellious. He held his grudge in silence. Instead of addressing the issue, he became a rebel. The more rebellious he became, the worse his company performed.

Jerry started making progress slowly. His team held meetings while he was absent. This allowed his direct reports to engage and collaborate with each other to solve the issues at hand.

Due to his high level of control and lack of agility, Jerry had extremely low levels of flexibility and innovation. He needed to let his direct reports find the solutions. He needed to let them make their own mistakes. He began to empower them to make decisions on their own. The result was that agility, creativity, and innovation began to improve. New ideas were generated to solve old problems. By letting go of personal control, Jerry confronted his fear of failure and became a more effective leader. He empowered his people, and they repaid him.

Jerry's transcendent leadership journey began when he faced himself and took responsibility and accountability for his behaviors and impact. As a result, his business unit began to perform better.

A leadership journey: Chuck's story

"Real change is difficult at the beginning, but gorgeous at the end. Change begins the moment you get the courage and step outside your comfort zone; change begins at the end of your comfort zone."

—**Roy T. Bennett**, *Light in the Heart*

People want to follow *people,* not *managers.* People want to be guided and inspired by leaders who are reachable, touchable, compassionate, honest, transparent, authentic, and "human." People want to learn from leaders who are smart and willing to mentor them. When reporting to leaders like these, employees generally *thrive* versus *survive.* They put their heart and soul into making the company successful.

For leaders to exhibit these types of behaviors, they need to develop wisdom that requires mastering the inner workings of one's own mind, heart, body, emotions, and soul. It is a journey few leaders take.

The story of Chuck is different from the story of Jerry. When I met him, Chuck was the CEO of a mid-sized insurance company later bought by a global organization. After the acquisition, he moved to the head of human resources of the holding company, with global responsibilities. Chuck wasn't done growing. He later became the CEO and Chairman of the Board of a large financial services company, a position he held until his retirement. When I met him the first time, what intrigued me most was his self-effacing humility and caring for his people. On top of that, he was incredibly intelligent and used his intuition wisely.

Chuck's business touch came from his years of experience in the financial services industry. That's where he'd honed his industry smarts and developed a high level of business acumen.

But he had more than that. He was emotionally intelligent. He had great business knowledge combined with heart. He had that personal touch with his people. He sensed what people were feeling and truly cared about them. His human touch differentiated him from many other leaders. This made him a stronger leader who held people accountable for their actions and results. He knew his shareholders expected results, and he was committed to giving them full value for his team's efforts.

But what he did was establish principles that gave his people the opportunity to excel. He treated everyone equally, looking past sex, race, religion, and gender to elevate people purely on merit. The diversity of the group, and their willingness to work together, led to its success.

Chuck believed in giving people second chances, too. He learned this principle when he was a young man early in his business career. He made a $10,000,000 mistake. When he recognized the mistake, he offered his resignation to the CEO of the company.

Somewhat surprising to him, the boss refused his resignation, saying, "Why would I let you go when I just spent $10 million training you?" This was a major turning point for Chuck. His boss believed in him. He acknowledged the mistake but was given a second chance. He never forgot that experience.

Chuck's success in business was a direct result of his being tough but caring, demanding but compassionate, and strict but enabling. He was a REAL person, deeply human, and that's what made him a good mentor and a good leader.

Chuck is humble and not ego-driven. He is willing to admit his mistakes. That is what drew people close to him and instilled passionate loyalty in them. He listened to other people's points of view but challenged their thinking to help them grow. Chuck had the self-confidence and inner strength to empower others in his organization to be their best.

The first step of the journey is awareness

It is easy to go off the rails. We all have limitations that keep us from achieving what we want to achieve. Our self-confidence can become unfounded pride or arrogance if we're not careful. Our concerns can become debilitating fears. Successes can over-inflate our egos, and failures can pop our balloons and leave us helpless to face the next challenges. We fail to be resilient. We make excuses. We don't bounce back. We fail to be REAL with ourselves and with others. We admit nothing. The biggest factor holding us back? We don't change.

We should endeavor to be more like Chuck than Jerry. We need to wake up to our personal problems, misgivings, insecurities, and defense mechanisms and find a way to peel back the onion as early as possible. We should become self-aware and proactive to change and grow.

The challenges to becoming a REAL leader are many and varied and require deep self-examination to recognize and address. The next chapter will help by pointing out some of the reasons that leaders go astray and why they derail. If leaders remain unconscious and unaware of their shortcomings, they will have a negative effect, not only on themselves but on their organization's short- and long-term success. Becoming a REAL leader is the only way to ensure a permanently healthy organization that has a lasting future.

CHAPTER 2

DERAILING AND GOING OFF-COURSE

"If you change yourself, you will change your world. If you change how you think then you will change how you feel and what actions, you take. And so, the world around you will change."

—Ghandi

Have you ever received feedback that you are too aggressive? That you need to take care of the people as well as drive for results? You need to speak up. Not everyone works the same as you and that you need to be more flexible in your approach as a leader? That you need to trust your people more and let go of control? That you need to understand which battles to fight versus fighting every battle? That you don't deal with conflict directly and you cover up too much for your people, that you are too protective?

As an executive coach to many senior leaders, I've seen witnessed the impact of these types of leadership behaviors. I've observed the difference between highly successful leaders and those who derail their careers. Provided that the leader has the business skills and capabilities, what differentiates highly successful leaders and those who derail tends to be fear and lack of awareness of the deeper drivers behind derailment behavior. Additionally, even when leaders receive the same feedback over and over again, they may not know how to change. Some leaders' fear that, if they change too much, they may fail. And yet, if they keep repeating the same behavior, they will fail. During this chapter, I hope to illustrate how fear creates derailing behaviors and how to start the change process.

In 1990 when my husband, Barry, and I started our company, Stop At Nothing, we were excited and terrified at the same time. We had a young family we needed to support and no skills or capabilities in the leadership and organizational development field. Barry had been previously married. With four children, he needed to make significant child support payments. Prior to starting Stop At Nothing, we worked together at a local bank and had a financially stable life. In early 1989, the bank announced that our banking employer was being merged with another bank, and Barry immediately announced Stop At Nothing.

At that time, many of our family and friends thought we were crazy. They warned us against doing something so risky. We would hear things like:

"You have kids to support."

"What if you fail?"

"How are you going to make your mortgage payment and survive?"

"You don't have any expertise in this field; you don't know what you are doing."

"Do you have a year's worth of money set aside?"

One of the things we learned about moving out of our comfort zone and taking risks is that in life, you must face your fears head-on. Barry and I didn't delude ourselves about our skills, experience, or the monumental task we had ahead of us. We knew the odds were stacked against us. What we did have was an inspirational dream with real possibility. We knew we would have to work hard to get there, and even though it was risky, the dream outweighed the risk.

One of the keys to transcending fear and moving beyond limitations is a having a meaningful, definite purpose with a deep desire to do something different. Barry and I both knew that if we did not take this chance and at least try, we would regret it for the rest of our lives. Dr. Susan Jeffers has a wonderful book entitled *Feel the Fear and Do It Anyway*. The book, with its ambitious title, "Feel the fear and do it anyway" became our mantra in the early days of Stop At Nothing. Our mission and purpose for Stop At Nothing now is the same as it was when we first started. We wanted to change the world by working with organizations to build a more humane, compassionate, and transparent workplace. We wanted to help build organizational cultures that recognized and valued differences between people. We believe that by creating conscious cultures, organizations can become more profitable. We recognized that many organizations lose money and margin because they didn't balance the equation between people, process, and the drive for results.

When we started our Stop At Nothing business, very

kind and loving people would tell us we had our heads in the clouds. Barry and I look back now, 30 years later, and often say, "Thank God we took the leap." I am proud to say we never missed a child support payment. Sure, there were times of peanut butter and jelly, but we never went hungry. We always had a roof over our heads, cars to drive, and vacations to take as a family.

At any point, we could have given up the Stop At Nothing dream and gone back to our banking careers, but the passion we had behind our purpose over-rode any fear we had. Recently, my husband and I started a new company, Conscious Business Insights, and we find ourselves facing the unknown once again. Some of our friends applauded us for taking the risk while others have asked, "Why are you doing this? You are so close to retirement. You have comfort and financial stability; new businesses take a lot of energy and work." But Barry and I say, "We have a dream and a mission and purpose we want to fulfill." Therefore, we started again.

Operating off-course

Everyone has unconscious, off-purpose, derailing behaviors. We have habits and patterns that we are unaware of. We affect others positively and negatively. When we are stressed, whether it is chronic or a result of a recent event, we behave in ways designed to protect and defend. Sometimes, these behaviors sabotage our efforts for success. When we operate from stress, we derail and go off-course. Whenever we are faced with a new challenge, uncertainty and fear can become the driver of our experience. If we feel we are outside of our comfort zone, heading into the unknown and don't know what to do, that often brings fear. In my years of working with people, I found that many do not recognize how fear operates in their lives. If we don't recognize how fear operates within us, we will derail our leadership effectiveness and, with it, our hopes and dreams.

All stress-related behaviors are driven by our survival instinct. That's how our biology is wired. At some point in our lives, we experience hardship, traumatic events, life-defining moments, and overwhelming situations. It is from those life-defining moments that we create beliefs, intentions, and emotional drivers that determine our behavioral response. Once we establish our reaction to these life-defining moments, which consist of beliefs, thoughts, and emotional drivers linked to behaviors, our reactions become programmed habits. Over time, these habits become unconscious only to be triggered when we face similar situations. Our unconscious minds dig through the filing cabinet of experiences, which cause us to react and apply our learned behavioral patterns again.

Generally, when we are stressed, we react out of our ingrained survival nature. It does not matter whether the situation is truly life-or-death or whether the situation is simply emotionally difficult. The mind and body react together under stress. Our defensive, stress-related behaviors become reflexive and unconscious. These behaviors are generally what we call leadership derailers.

Becoming conscious is the antidote to the poison of unconscious derailment behavior. Consciousness is a fundamental leadership skill. It's about being in the present moment. Without conscious awareness, we are unable to see reality for what it is and are unable to adapt. Many leaders fail because they are unaware of their strengths and weaknesses and, as a result, they fail to adapt and modify their leadership approach.

Many organizations—for the same reason—fail because senior leaders don't create conscious and aware cultures. As a result, they don't adapt. This happens because leadership either doesn't see the signs or they ignore the ones that require change. This is unconsciousness. When we bring to light our negative conditioning and fully comprehend the impact of our derailment behavior, we begin the journey on the road to healing, enlightenment, and awareness.

Having a beginner's mind and learning from our negative experiences opens the gateway to inner freedom and develops wisdom. Having a beginner's mind means being able to suspend immediate judgment and look at feedback and information in a new way. Leaders who are unconscious and asleep are unable to see reality as it is. They see reality as they want to see it. Consider Jerry; his first defense is to aggressively blame, deny, and defend his position and behaviors. He doesn't have a beginner's mind. His reactions show his need to be right. He shuts down others' ideas.

As an executive coach, I've seen this type of behavior many times. Eventually, Jerry and others like him hit the glass ceiling and because they have not developed their emotional intelligence, they often do not reach the pinnacle of the career they desire.

What about leaders who blame, deny, and defend but

do it nicely? It's still the same result as Jerry. I've witnessed this repeatedly when working to transform organizational cultures. Out of respect for others, leaders don't challenge in an appropriate way, and organizations end up with a group of leaders who unconsciously collaborate to keep the status quo by suppressing feedback. Learning to transcend our fight or flight response, however, is the gateway to transcendent leadership.

The fight or flight response

No one escapes life without having negative or difficult life events. We all face rejection, embarrassment, betrayal, and failure. We've had our hearts broken and acted in ways that we regret. When we encounter difficult situations, it is natural and normal for our fight or flight response to kick in. We react based on our stress-response. Our stress-related behaviors are developed from our past life experiences. When we are in fight or flight mode, it is difficult to be creative, agile and innovative.

Depending on your programmed responses, you will unconsciously pick a pre-programmed behavioral response versus being proactive and making a choice. The fight or flight response leads to one of three actions: flight, fight, or freeze. Or as author Neal Shusterman so eloquently puts it, "Fight, flight, and screw up royally."

REAL leadership means we face the deeper programs behind our fight or flight response so that we can reprogram ourselves. Defensive structures are built over time and reaffirmed and used throughout our lives even when the event that created the defensive behavior is in the distant past. Because our defensive structures are a significant part of us, we say things like, "That's just the way I am." But, it's not. We must take responsibility. We made up the behavior, the belief, and the emotion that drives the behavior. We are the master programmer of our mental, emotional, and behavioral responses. The sooner we recognize this and do something about it, the better. This is why self-awareness is the foundation for leadership success.

Overcoming stress-related derailment behaviors begins with these three steps:

- Self-awareness
- Self-regulation and self-management
- Self-change

Self-regulation and self-management start the change process. Self-change means we rewrite our programs rather than merely manage our responses. When we rewrite our programs, we change and transcend the definition of who we think we are.

Businesses now recognize the importance of emotional intelligence, self-awareness, and self-change. Think *360 surveys* and *cultural and engagement surveys*. Businesses are measuring the impact of leadership behavior as it relates to engagement, culture, brand, reputation, and organizational results. Businesses are investing billions in executive coaching and leadership development all with a single purpose—to change behavior.

Leadership derailers

*"Whether you prevail or fail, endure or die, depends more on what **you do** to yourself than on **what the world does** to you."*

—**Jim Collins,** *How the Mighty Fall*

What Jerry learned is that he had leadership blind spots. If he doesn't change his perspective and accept responsibility for the reality he created, he will likely derail his goal of becoming the CEO of the holding company he worked for. In Jerry's case, it is easy to identify his derailing behaviors. Jerry is not a conscious and REAL leader; in fact, he is an unconscious manager.

REAL leaders have healthy self-awareness, know how to self-manage and self-regulate, and maintain an inner state of well-being. REAL leaders know how to engage with others, drive collaboration and alignment, and help other leaders grow. They are agile, innovative, and flexible in their approach. They are not afraid to admit they are wrong and don't have all the answers. Finally, REAL leaders are humble, authentic, ethical, compassionate, transparent, and trustworthy. They are driven by a greater sense of purpose and meaning for the greater good of the community versus being driven by their ego and self-centeredness. In Jerry's case, he is driven by ego-based fears: the need to be right, and self-centeredness.

The reasons leaders fail

There are eight major reasons that leaders derail. These are underlying drivers that leaders may not be aware of.

They:
1. Lack awareness of their derailment behavior.
2. Are driven by pride and ego. They are defensive and continually shift blame to others.
3. Have a need to control everything. They can be outright control freaks or control through passive-aggressive tendencies.
4. Operate from fear. They act or avoid doing things based on fear.
5. Have deeply ingrained personality traits and characteristics that negatively impact their leadership behaviors and style that they may or may not recognize.
6. Are perfectionists.
7. Are narcissistic—leaders who need to be the center of attention, and lead by my *way or the highway* ethos. These leaders tend to have an inflated view of themselves.
8. Are moody and tend to over-react and become melodramatic.

When leaders are consciously or unconsciously driven by these types of inner drivers and motives, their leadership behavior and effectiveness are compromised. As a result, how they collaborate, engage, communicate, and align with others will be compromised. Then, their ability to incorporate new ideas, to be flexible, and to promote other people's ideas are also diminished. When leaders operate from these derailment motives and drivers, their leadership becomes less effective.

The ways leaders fail

There are many leadership derailment behaviors. Based on years of consulting and working with leaders, I've found that there are 10 major derailment behaviors. Leaders can derail even if they exhibit only one of these behaviors. Many times, leaders who derail exhibit 2-4 of these behaviors. Leaders who derail:

1. Micromanage and control.
2. Freeze and become tentative, slowing down the decision-making process.
3. Need to be right.
4. Lack teamwork, collaboration, and integration.
5. Exhibit lone-wolf behavior.
6. Think they know it all.
7. Have paralysis by analysis.
8. Are bullies; they domineer, control, and exhibit aggressive behavior.
9. Lack a vision and strategy.
10. Lack transparency.

All of these behaviors are based in fear. REAL leadership is about developing a healthy relationship with fear, not avoiding fear. We are humans, and humans have fear. The more we acknowledge how fear operates within us, the freer we become to be more proactive and creative in our leadership style.

Scott Keller and Colin Price, in their book *Beyond Performance*, discuss the experience of Pixar Studios as a good example of how an organization handles risk and protects against derailers. The company is a creative enterprise with hundreds of professionals involved in every film project. Any one of them can come up with a great idea at any time. In encouraging new ideas and creativity, the studio recognizes uncertainty and fear as a way of doing business effectively.

The philosophy at Pixar is "If we aren't always at least a little bit scared, we're not doing our job." The studio is in the business of producing something new each time they begin a film project. So, the studio puts itself at risk. It has produced many films, including one about a robot in a world full of trash (*WALL-E*) and one about a French rat who wants to be a chef (*Ratatouille*). There was risk in making each one of these films, but the studio took chances and was rewarded with commercial success.

Pixar felt that, to be original, they had to take risks, knowing that if they failed, they could recover because they had talented people. Management's job was not to prevent risk but to accept it and build in the capability to recover when failure occurred. The company established a culture where it was safe to tell the truth, to challenge all assumptions, to try different approaches, and to take risks every day. And who is management? Management is the leaders. Therefore, it is the leader's job not to prevent risk but to accept it and build in the capability to recover when crisis and failure occurs.

Whether we are conscious of our fears or not, we can still be driven by fear. The problem with fear, if we have not recognized and mastered it, is that we won't have the resilience to recover when failure occurs. Fear can lead to risk avoidance and bad judgment. For leaders to wake-up, the first step is to overcome fear-driven behaviors.

Fear

Fear is the most unrecognized and unconscious driver of leadership behavior. It is like a stealth bomber; it sneaks up on us without a sound, and before we know it, we operate out of fear. It causes contraction. When we are afraid, we become hyper-focused and constricted in our thinking. When we are afraid, our decisions are generally made out of our survival instincts.

Although fear is a powerful force designed to protect you from danger, it can constrain you and prevent you from reaching your goals. Fear of failure impacts the way we view situations and the way we act, respond, set goals, and pursue our dreams. Fear can become a hidden barrier to success. There are many types of fears. The common fears I've witnessed when coaching leaders are:

1. Being seen as an imposter or a fraud.
2. Making tough decisions or fear of being wrong.
3. Taking criticism.
4. Losing control or being in over your head.
5. Conflict.
6. Risk-taking – expanding the comfort zone.
7. Rejection.
8. Success.
9. Making someone angry.
10. Standing up and speaking out.
11. Being demoted.
12. Being laid off.
13. Financial ruin or instability.

The fear list can go on and on. Often, fear gets hidden or smoothed over by rationalization and logic. Fear is the greatest obstacle to getting things done. REAL leaders learn to face, leverage, and transcend fear. They become fearless by mastering fear.

A recent survey by the social network *Linkagoal* found that fear of failure is the number one reason that people will not set goals or try something new. Fear of failure was a major derailer for 31% of the 1,083 adult respondents to the study, a larger percentage than those who feared spiders (30%), experiencing the paranormal (15%), or being home alone (9%) (Peg Moline, 2015).

> *"Fearlessness is not the absence of fear.*
> *It's the mastery of fear. It's about getting up one more*
> *time than we fall down."*
> **—Arianna Huffington**

Highly effective and inspirational leaders are afraid, but they face and admit their fear and move beyond it. They are aware of their behaviors that are driven by fear. This is humility and humanness. REAL leaders have the courage to admit their vulnerabilities and the behaviors associated with them and know how to make purposeful change to their leadership behaviors. As Arianna Huffington stated, it's all about learning to master fear. Fear is an important messenger; it lets us know we are about to expand our comfort zone. Fear gives us the opportunity to transform or to stay the course and maintain the status quo.

I received a call from a family-owned financial services company. They have been in business nearly 50 years with a strong brand and reputation for honesty and being customer oriented. About 10 years ago, the family decided to hire outside management to run the business. The owners created a family board to guide the new CEO and ensure the values they instilled in the company stayed. The new CEO started in 2012 and began to grow the business.

The CEO, Angela, called because she needed help with one of their strongest people. Their Head of Sales, Martha, aged 36, was hired in 2014. She was a go-getter and increased revenues over 300% in just four years. Everyone was excited about her strategic capability, energy, and capacity to build strong relationships with their client base.

Although Angela and the board knew Martha had issues as a team player, they were willing to overlook these issues because Martha was such a high sales producer. Martha was known as a bully and a name dropper. She would use her position to gain power over others. She would lose her temper if her peers or direct reports didn't respond as quickly as she wanted. Martha was not a detailed communicator. She often miscommunicated because she was too high-level in her communication style. When she didn't get what she needed or wanted, she would blame others rather than owning her side of the issue–poor communication.

Despite her communication issues, Martha continued to increase revenue. However, her behavior became more problematic. Her peers no longer wanted to work with her, and long-term high-performing employees were leaving the company. There was concern from the board that if they let Martha go, the business would stop growing and lose market share they had gained as a result of Martha's sales skills. The CEO and the board were afraid that if they fired Martha, she could take the book of business and go to work for a competitor. Four years after Martha started, she had her eyes on the CEO role. She felt she had proven her worth and that she deserved the role. Angela and the board knew Martha was not ready for the position.

Angela knew that Martha needed to improve her emotional intelligence skills if she was ever going to get promoted. Her leadership 360 assessment revealed several blind spots:

1. Bullying behavior.
2. Blaming: never owning her side of a mistake.
3. Aggressiveness: being pushy and domineering to get her way.
4. Demeaning: treating others without respect.
5. Denying and Defending: inability to acknowledge her impact on others.

When Martha received her feedback, her immediate response was, "They don't understand me." When Angela pressed the issue, Martha then blamed her peers and direct reports for being incompetent, forcing her to do everything, so she didn't have time for "niceties." Angela pushed again, acknowledging Martha's high sales performance and her role in growing the business. Angela assured Martha she could continue in her role as a high sales performer. But if her unacceptable behavior continued, she would never be considered a successor for the CEO role. This only infuriated Martha more and led to further defensiveness.

Angela took the time to explain that if Martha didn't improve her emotional intelligence, she would find herself in the same situation in another company. Angela pressed Martha to take the feedback seriously so that she would have the opportunity to change.

> *"There's only so much change you can affect if you are not aware of what needs changing to begin with."*
> —**Jeff Boss,** *Why Leaders Derail, Forbes Magazine*

Antidotes to Fear

Fear, when transcended, can become the catalyst we need to transform and transcend our own boundaries. One antidote to fear mentioned earlier is having a major definite purpose in life. Other antidotes for fear are consciousness, resilience, and self-awareness. Self-awareness is key to recognizing fear, and resilience helps to transcend fear. Resilience is the ability to bounce back and the ability to recover quickly from difficult times and stressful conditions. Resilience is the ability to adapt rather than react based on habit and defense.

To develop cognitive and emotional resilience, along with emotional intelligence, starts with revisiting past life-defining moments to release the emotional glue that holds derailment behavioral patterns in place. In Chapter 3, we will discuss in detail how to develop resilience, release the emotional glue that causes us to derail, and create more freedom and choice.

CHAPTER 3

LEADERSHIP RESILIENCE

*"No matter how you define success, you will need to
be resilient, empowered, authentic,
and limber to get there."*

—Joanie Connell, Flying Without a Helicopter

Resilience is the foundation of wisdom. It is developed from
our innate capacity to heal and bounce back from our
psychological and emotional wounds and traumas. No-one
escapes fear, anger, pain, and suffering. We all face hardship
and difficult times. During tough times, resilience is the
courage and strength of our spirit to recover and heal
ourselves. When we heal ourselves, we find inner peace and
harmony.

A more formal definition of resilience is the ability to
bounce back or recover quickly after hardship, conflict,
difficulties, and stressful times. Our resilience is tested every
day. From the on-going challenges of dealing with our
personal relations, work life, raising children, paying our
debts, and creating financial stability to the more difficult
challenges of crises, physical and emotional illness, and

death. It is during these times we draw upon the strength of our inner resources to bounce back and pull us through. In this section, we explore how to develop our inner resources and spiritual strength to improve leadership resilience.

We need resilience to survive; otherwise, we emotionally fall apart, making it difficult to move forward in our lives. Our resilience is impacted by how we perceive, interpret, and emotionally process the events around us. How we interpret and process our experience is dependent on our belief systems, how we think, and how we feel. What we believe, think, and feel about any given situation can trigger an internal stress response (our fight or flight mode) or trigger the relaxation response.

Resilience is how well we manage our stress and relaxation response. When faced with sudden change and unpredictability, resilience is the foundation of agility and flexibility. When confronted with overwhelming circumstance and fear, we draw upon courage. When we suffer and feel pain, we find resilience through the strength of our spirit. For many, when faced with challenging times, we draw on the strength of Spirit to guide us through and help us recover. Learning how to reprogram our stress-response helps to develop our internal spiritual strength and courage.

Developing resilience starts with self-awareness. We need deep self-awareness to identify our underlying beliefs, thoughts, and feelings that drive our actions and reactions. We need to know when we are in or out of balance within ourselves. In yogic traditions, being in or out of balance depends on two forces: the force of stability (*sthira*) and the force of surrender (*sukha*). *Sthira* refers to grounded steadiness and strength in action, whereas *sukha* refers to ease and peace by letting go and surrendering.

Sthira etymologically is derived from the root, *stha* which means "to take a stand." As a life-practice, it means we are strong, firm, active, grounded, and steady. *Sukha*, when literally translated means *good place*. *Su* equals *good,* and *kha* means *place*. As a life-practice, it means being in a good, peaceful, and joyful place within, experiencing comfort and acceptance with what is. Each aspect can become out of balance. We need to know when we are driving too hard, being too active, and too pushy versus when we are being too soft, and not confronting the issues facing us. Deeper self-awareness means we know what drives us in one direction or the other. Leadership wisdom means we can use our resilience and change. This section helps you learn to uncover and discover the beliefs that underlie these forces and start the process of change. It is when we find balance between these two forces that we find inner peace and harmony.

Leadership resilience is the foundation of wisdom and knowing how and when to apply these two forces. When is steady, grounded action required, and when do you let go and not fight every battle? Knowing when to apply these forces starts with emotional intelligence, self-awareness, and self-management.

There are four characteristics of leadership resilience that, if focused on and developed, can help you lower stress levels, develop inner strength and courage, find inner spiritual strength, and improve your leadership effectiveness.

The four qualities of leadership resilience are:
1. Self-Awareness: Unconsciousness and Life-Defining Moments
2. Cognitive and emotional intelligence
3. Self-management
4. Well-being

We improve our inner state of being by improving our resilience. We lead from a more grounded and steady state with less fear. Leaders who exhibit high resilience tend to have more highly engaged and innovative teams. Start developing your inner spiritual strength by learning to develop these four leadership qualities.

Self-awareness

Becoming more self-aware is a lifelong journey. Depending on the day, I spend 1.5 to 2.5 hours in the morning meditating and practicing yoga. I've been practicing meditation and mindfulness for over 40 years. Meditation helps me increase my self-awareness, improve my resilience, and decrease my stress response. When meditating, I let go of emotional baggage that I may be carrying and open myself to new ideas and creative ways to solve the problems I am facing. I find meditation and yoga to be as important as eating right and staying fit. Without emotionally centering myself, I become more susceptible to derailing behaviors.

Recently, I went through one of the most emotionally challenging times in my life. My father passed in June 2017. My dear friend, mentor, teacher, and mother died during the eclipse on August 21, 2017. A month later, my uncle died. I also had normal stresses running the Stop At Nothing business. In early April 2018, we got word that my brother-in-law was diagnosed with Stage IV pancreatic cancer and he had less than four months to live. My husband's grandmother passed away in early May. Then, in July 2018, we restructured Stop At Nothing and formed two companies, Conscious Business Insights and Stop At Nothing. In the meantime—alongside all the normal stresses of everyday life —I was going home to be with my sister and her husband every few weeks. I felt it was important to be physically, emotionally, and spiritually present. While I wouldn't want to go back and change my behavior, these were trying times.

To help manage my stress, I stuck with my morning meditation and yoga practices. I felt I was handling the stress well. I thought my meditative practice, herbs, and vitamin consumption were enough. In August 2018, I had an executive physical at the Cleveland Clinic and found out I had hypertension with my blood pressure readings at 140/100. I was blown away. My normal blood pressure runs in the range of 100/65 to 110/75. I've never had a blood pressure reading like that. Talk about a wake-up call. Funny, I was telling everyone my heart physically hurt. I never imagined I was developing hypertension and yet, my body was trying to tell me something was wrong. This is the importance of self-awareness.

On one hand, intellectually, I knew I was stressed. Although I practice self-awareness on a daily basis, I was *unaware* of how the stress was impacting my health. I was given a choice by the doctor: de-stress or take medication for hypertension. My life was not going to change. My brother-in-law was still dying. I was still going to make the 6.5-hour trip back and forth to Cleveland. I still had a job to do, clients that needed my help, and my own life to lead. What I had to do was 1) become more aware of the deeper drivers of how the stress was impacting me, 2) change my relationship with those deeper drivers, and 3) let go.

That day at the Cleveland Clinic, as I went from appointment to appointment, I didn't read, do emails, or watch television. I stopped, meditated, and deeply felt what was going on inside of me. I was over-doing sthira. I was trying to be strong and hold it together. I had not deeply faced the depth of sorrow of losing my brother-in-law and my other family members. I needed to balance by practicing sukha, by allowing, accepting, and feeling the pain of my loss.

Although sukha means good place, if I didn't allow myself to open up and accept my sorrow and grief, if I stayed strong, I would not find inner peace and build strength of spirit. I could have pushed through and remained strong, but at the rate I was going, that strategy was adversely impacting my heart. So, there I was, at the Cleveland Clinic sitting between appointments, letting go of my grief and crying. By the end of the day, my blood pressure tested 120/80. My choice was to lower my internal reaction to stress rather than take blood pressure medication. Now, five months later, my average blood pressure is 110/75.

For anyone who's watched someone fade away with cancer, you know in your heart how painful it is. I've known my brother-in-law, Tony, for nearly 35 years. My sister, Tony, and I lived together when we were young and starting out in life. Watching him waste away from the cancer was unbearable. My circumstances didn't change, but I changed the way I responded to my circumstances.

To find my inner balance and decrease my blood pressure permanently, I had to dig deeper, peel back the onion, and become more self-aware. I was *unaware* of the biological impact of the stress and sorrow. None of us are perfect. All of us have aspects of awareness and unawareness. To improve and develop your self-awareness skills, you need to:

1. Meditate.
2. Make the unconscious conscious.
3. Dive into deep self-inquiry.
4. Use moments of truth.

Learning to fully face our challenges mentally, emotionally, physically, and spiritually means deepening our self-awareness, allowing us to make purposeful changes. In my case, the realization and wake-up call of my blood pressure allowed me to create an inner transformation of my thoughts, beliefs, and emotions to get back to being deeply grounded and centered within myself. Without self-awareness, there is no opportunity for change.

Unconscious behaviors, meditation, and deep self-inquiry

Meditation is the practice of stilling our mind and becoming centered within. Through meditation, we can make the unconscious conscious and become more aware of our underlying emotional drivers of behavior. When we become more aware of our deeper drivers, we begin to improve our emotional intelligence.

According to Daniel Goleman, "emotional intelligence consists of self-awareness, self-regulations, social skills, and empathy." An effective leader knows that, in today's world, it takes more than business skills, intelligence, and competencies to drive organizational results and reach the highest levels in career growth. REAL Leadership combines emotional intelligence and business intelligence for improved personal and professional success.

Self-awareness is more than simply understanding personality traits; it includes understanding the triggers of the emotional drivers behind repetitive non-productive behaviors, such as fear of failure, fear of conflict, anger, anxiety, and the need to please. Many leaders derail because 1) they don't have enough self-awareness to understand the drivers behind adverse leadership behaviors and 2) they don't know how to change their behaviors. When leaders make the unconscious conscious through understanding their emotional drivers, the opportunity to change their behavior increases. Self-awareness does not guarantee behavioral change, but it is a prerequisite for it.

Meditation is one tool to increase self-awareness. Another tool is feedback. Feedback from your family, friends, co-workers, boss, and employees also makes the unconscious conscious. My blood pressure was feedback. The opportunity to listen to and learn from feedback is endless. At work, we can receive 360 feedback, culture and engagement surveys to help us understand our behaviors and the impact we are having on people. Our family and friends give us feedback and emotional support. In both cases, at work and at home, we may act on the feedback, or we may disregard and not believe it.

"By three methods we may learn wisdom: first, by reflection, which is noblest; second, by imitation, which is easiest; and third, by experience, which is the most bitter."

—Confucius

Sometimes in life, we run so fast trying to get things done that we don't stop and reflect on what we are doing and why we are doing it. Deep self-reflection and inquiry are tools to make the unconscious conscious. Self-inquiry and self-reflection mean we examine our inner world of beliefs, thoughts, and emotional habit patterns. When we examine our inner world, we look at *what* we do and *why* we think the way we do. The first step is reflecting on *what* we do. Take a moment now and reflect on some examples of *what* questions:

1. What worries me the most?
2. What am I really afraid of?
3. What am I holding onto that I can't let go of?
4. What matters most to me in my life?
5. Reflect on a difficult conversation that ended badly. What happened? What did you think, believe, say and do?

To further peel back the onion and find the deeper

emotional drivers behind your behaviors, take the *what* questions through a second phase of self-inquiry. Take some time now to ask and reflect upon these important *why* questions:

1. What worries me the most? Why does it worry me? How do I behave because of my worries? Why is it important to behave and act this way? What would happen if I don't? Is what I believe necessarily true? Is there another perspective and another truth?

2. What am I really afraid of? Why am I afraid? How does fear show up in my leadership and in my relationships? Is what I believe necessarily true? Is there another perspective and another truth?

3. What am I holding onto that I can't let go of? Why is it important to hold on? What would happen if I let go? Why would letting go be a good or bad thing? How does this drive my behavior? Is what I believe necessarily true? Is there another perspective and another truth?

4. What matters most to me in my life? Why is this important to me? Am I living in accordance with what matters most? If no, why not? How do I behave when I am not living in accordance with my value? If I am living in alignment with what is most important to me, how do I behave in a way that demonstrates my values? Is what I believe necessarily true? Is there another perspective and another truth?

5. Have I had a difficult conversation that ended badly? What happened? What did I think, believe,

say and do? Why do I think and believe this way? Why is it important for me to act this way? What would happen if I decided to change? Is what I believe necessarily true? Is there another perspective and another truth?

By answering these questions, we deepen our self-awareness. This is the first step to creating change in your life. Using meditation and self-reflection you make the unconscious conscious, gaining deeper awareness and providing the platform for change. Next, is to peel back the onion a little more and learn how we developed the beliefs and behaviors we outlined in the previous exercise. Beliefs, tied to thoughts and emotions, are the foundation of our actions and guidelines for our behavior.

Life defining moments and our sense of worth

Life is like a roller coaster; we go through many ups and downs. Sometimes, the ride is thrilling, and other times, the ride is downright scary. Sometimes, we are glad when the ride is over, and others of us want to get back on the ride again. These ups and downs, the joys and sorrows, help us to create and define our belief structures. When we go through painful life experiences, they become defining moments for us. During those experiences, we create defensive behaviors designed to help and protect us.

Most think being defensive is a bad thing. However, we need protection, just like we need help and support. We need to emotionally protect ourselves. Without fear and defense, we could not emotionally and psychologically survive. Defenses are protection. The problem is that defensive structures are constructed for a particular experience at a specific moment in time. When we create a defensive structure, many times, that defensive structure becomes the unconscious foundation for behaviors that can last a lifetime.

We get our heart broken, and we may decide to always protect our heart. We may make a vow that we will never allow ourselves to get hurt again. Then, we wonder why we have difficulty with future relationships and intimacy. A defensive structure for a particular moment has now become a guiding belief for all our relationships. We fear rejection. The same is true for betrayal. At one point or another, we will experience betrayal. When we experience betrayal, we sometimes, later in life, develop trust issues. We may create a belief and make a vow, saying "I will never trust people again." At some point, we will experience failure. During the most painful part of that failure, we may make a commitment, create a belief, and take a vow to make sure we will never fail again. Sometimes, fear of failure beliefs results in a lack of trust, micro-management, power-plays, low self-confidence, and the need to be right.

Positive life experiences help us form positive beliefs about ourselves and the world around us. Positive life-defining moments become the foundation of our sense of worth, self-confidence, and self-esteem. They help us to mold our strengths as people and as leaders.

Forming beliefs from our life experiences is how we become the programmer of our lives. If we have patterns that cause us to derail, there is a deep belief and emotion behind the behavior. If we have patterns that create success and happiness, there is also a deep belief and emotion driving those patterns of behavior. To increase self-awareness, it is important to uncover the beliefs contained within the operating system of our brain. To begin to uncover your deeper underlying beliefs that drive your behavior, you may want to self-reflect on the following questions:

1. How can I create more work-life balance? What beliefs do I have that allow me to create balance? What beliefs do I have that prevent me from creating balance? Are these beliefs necessarily true?

2. To what degree do I feel I am are the creator of my destiny in life? How do I feel about what I've created so far? What beliefs do I have about my ability to create my destiny? Do my beliefs hold me back or empower me?

3. What have I learned from my biggest mistake? What beliefs did I form in my life as a result of this mistake that are still in operation today? Do these beliefs still serve me? Do they hinder me?

4. What have I learned from my greatest triumph? What beliefs did I form in my life as a result of this success? Do these beliefs still serve me?

It is worth your time and effort to deeply explore the beliefs that underlie your behavior. So much of our behavior is driven by unconscious tendencies. If we take the time to explore, to peel back the onion and dig deeper, we often find beliefs that we can let go. This increases our energy, passion, and creativity. When we let go of beliefs that limit us in some way, we are free to explore something new. We may even find hidden beliefs and skills that we can bring into our lives, making us stronger and making us better people and leaders.

Cognitive and emotional intelligence

Building on a foundation of self-awareness, cognitive and emotional intelligence are tools that we can use and develop to help us reset our fight or flight response. All behaviors are programs we've adopted that consist of these components: beliefs, thoughts, emotions, behaviors, and results.

The major components of memory and repeated behaviors are beliefs, thoughts, emotions, and actions. The way we derail ourselves is keeping the memory alive. We keep memories and defensive behavioral patterns alive by replaying them over and over, like a song on repeat. We remember the event that happened to us, and we continue to believe the same beliefs, think the same thoughts, and feel the same way. When we play this over and over again, we program ourselves to repeat that behavioral pattern. It is easy to become patterned into thinking the same way about the same event and never change our perspective. We don't forgive, and we don't heal. To become cognitively and emotionally resilient, we must change how we perceive the events that happened to us and move on. If we don't like the results we are getting, we need to change one or more of the components related to the behavior.

I won't ever forget being physically, emotionally and sexually abused. I have, however, let go of my emotional attachment to the pain I experienced. The memories no longer haunt me emotionally. I gained inner strength as a result of pain. Through forgiveness, I opened my heart and learned to love and trust again. As a leader, this helped me to let go of my need to control everything and allow others to learn and grow.

We need cognitive intelligence to change the beliefs we developed as a result of our life's difficulties. We need emotional intelligence to let go of the emotional glue that holds defensive habit patterns in place. Leadership resilience is built on cognitive and emotional intelligence. Going hand in hand, resilience impacts our cognitive and emotional intelligence. They are interdependent. Studies show that stress negatively impairs cognitive and emotional intelligence. "Cognition is our ability to think, behave, and respond clearly in the face of sudden or chronic stress. Cognitive resilience is the ability to overcome negative effects of stress on cognitive functioning" (Staal et al. 2008). Cognitive intelligence is the ability to make sense of your surroundings and decide what to do. Cognitive resilience is the ability to re-formulate your beliefs and thoughts so that old emotional beliefs no longer trigger you.

Emotional intelligence is self-awareness, self-regulation, and your ability to read the mood of others. It means understand inner motivation and drivers, with compassion and empathy for yourself and others. Emotional resilience is the ability to bounce back after difficult events. What does this mean to you as a leader?

Using emotional intelligence, you identify the underlying emotions that drive your behavior. You uncover and discover deeper inner drivers and motives. Using emotional resilience, you let go of the emotional triggers based on past experience. When you let go of those emotions, it is much easier to change behavior. But it means really letting go. Many people hold on emotionally to events that occurred a long time ago. They understand cognitively what happened. They even say they have forgiven or gotten over the situation, but often, many people haven't let go of their emotional attachment to difficult events. When we don't let go of the emotional attachment, the impact of that emotion still operates in the background and subsequently impacts our behavior.

> *"Real change is difficult at the beginning, but gorgeous at the end. Change begins the moment you get the courage and step outside your comfort zone; change begins at the end of your comfort zone."*
> —**Roy T. Bennett**

When people move on, it generally means they have fully learned from the experience. They found the lesson. They have transcended the influence of their past and are now creating their future.

Self-management

When I became aware of my blood pressure, I had the opportunity to make a new choice about my behavior: either continue as I was or do something different. I was "managing" my situation with meditation, yoga, stress reduction, stillness, herbs, and vitamins. But I was not transcending the situation. Transcending my situation meant facing the deeper emotions of pain and deep sadness so that I could let them go.

When we are unaware and unconscious, we have no choice. We are destined to repeat the patterns of our past based on the emotional defensive structures and behaviors we developed a long time ago. When I was young, I developed a defensive structure called "be strong, be tough, don't let them see you as weak and most importantly, don't cry." This was the deeper belief structure in operation that drove up my blood pressure. I needed to be seen as strong and having it all together. It's wasn't until I had the strength and courage to be vulnerable that I was able to self-manage and change my behavior. Remember, I had a choice: de-stress or take blood pressure medication. I decided I would change my relationship to the stress I was experiencing.

What does this have to do with conscious leadership? What is self-management and why is it important in leadership and cultural effectiveness? Why is it important to understand our personal history and become aware?

Essentially, self-management involves emotional self-regulation. Emotional self-regulation is the ability to:

1. Understand the emotional drivers behind behavior
2. Know when the stress-response has been triggered
3. Change in the moment, moving from reacting to responding

Emotions are energy in motion, impacting and driving behaviors. There is an emotional component to all behavior. Even behavior we believe is based on logic has an emotional driver. This is how we are wired.

Understanding the underlying reason for behavior and then, having the ability to change, is emotional self-regulation. Emotionally, we are unconsciously driven to approach, avoid, or attack. Self-regulation starts with understanding how we emotionally respond, even if the emotional driver is unconscious.

If we are unaware, we *react* instead of *respond*. Identifying the underlying unconscious emotions requires becoming still and listening. Learning to be mindful and self-reflective develops self-awareness. With that foundation, you can self-regulate, self-manage, and change.

Well-being

Joe is a client of mine. One day, he called me to ask me questions on how to deal with his board. He had taken over a family-owned business and was the first outside leader to run this privately-owned company. As I sat and listened, I realized he was unbelievably stressed. When I asked him about his stress levels, he said he was fine. When I asked about his sleep, exercise, weight, and his emotional disposition, his answers gave him away. He was suffering from insomnia, had gained weight, was drinking more alcohol and coffee than ever before, felt more tired, and was constantly worried. After giving me all his physical ailments, he woke up and realized how stressed he was. Even though his wife had been telling him he was stressed, never home and giving up his life, he didn't believe her. Sitting together after he rattled everything off that was bothering him, he said, "I guess my wife is right; I am completely and totally stressed. How did this happen?"

When he came to me, he was trying to figure out better strategies to get more done in a shorter period of time. What I helped him to recognize was that he was killing himself to please the owners and not fail. He couldn't do any more or work any faster; it was physically impossible. Instead of standing up and pushing back, he stayed silent and tried harder. He was afraid of failing so he pushed himself to work harder and longer. In the meantime, he was not living in alignment with his deeper values of spending time with his family and watching his children grow.

So many of the leaders I work with struggle with work-life balance. They will put themselves last in order to empty their mailboxes, complete the next project, and achieve the next goal. But at what cost? Joe's health began to suffer, and he was missing out on self-renewal and time with family. Maintaining emotional well-being and balance is the key to a long and healthy life and good leadership. What does it mean to have physical and emotional well-being? How does one self-renew?

The World Health Organization defines well-being as "a state of complete physical, mental, and social well-being, and not merely the absence of disease or infirmity." In my client's case, he wasn't sick, but he was definitely headed for disease. He wasn't happy and felt like he was failing in his role at work, as a father, and as a husband. Like me, he thought he was handling everything well, but, as we peeled back the layers of his onion, he was struggling.

Emotional and physical well-being are interdependent. When we are emotionally out of balance and are not able to come back to center, ultimately, we become physically ill.

Emotional dis-ease is part of the physical stress response of the body. We experience physical disease—such as when we are sick, over-worked, stressed, and have a lot of tension—emotionally.

We can develop habits of insomnia, over/under-eating or over/under-exercising, and when this happens, we become physically out of balance, our immune system is compromised, and we develop disease, high blood pressure, and other stress-related illnesses.

Self-renewal consists of taking the time to physically and emotionally recharge. By stepping out of the daily fray, we can look at life and situations from a different perspective. This helps us to become more agile, innovative, and confident.

The question I kept asking Joe was, "Is it worth your life?" By the 10th time I asked him that question, he started to get it. First, he had to change his relationship to the situation. He needed to reframe his fear of failing and work with his cognitive and emotional intelligence. He needed to step back, meditate, and self-reflect. I gave him self-reflection homework, asking him to deeply look at what he was doing and why he was doing it. Why was he driving himself so hard that he stopped taking care of himself, and losing time with his family? What was driving him to think, believe and act this way? After doing the homework, he realized he had to reframe his definition of what failing meant to him. He came back to me with the realization that he was doing all he could and he wasn't a failure. He recognized that what the owners were asking him to do was impossible. Through meditation and self-reflection, he gained the courage he needed to take a stand and create a strategy to solve the issues.

The resilient leader has the self-confidence to handle difficult situations head-on and values the challenge to do so. These leaders have the energy and personality and the emotional stability to engage in problem-solving without being derailed along the way.

REAL leaders have the self-awareness and self-management skills that enable them to handle adversity with a certain comfort level. They use the leadership wisdom they have acquired to understand the effects of any problems in their organization and their teammates. They are empathetic to emotional strains on others and offer support to allay fears and sustain group resilience.

Many organizations set goals, train, and incentivize individuals to meet those goals. They encourage individual contributions for personal and career growth. But resilient organizations also foster open communication and risk-taking. They structure and restructure themselves to meet new objectives. They share decision-making. They employ individuals who can adapt to change and who react quickly, confidently, and constructively. These people can tolerate uncertainty.

Howard and Irving did research on resilience and wrote about its effects on leadership. Their work, "*The Impact of Obstacles and Developmental Experiences on Resilience in Leadership Formation,*" *was published in the Proceedings of the American Society for Business and Behavioral Sciences.* The research showed that leaders developed through active engagement in hardships or facing obstacles. By overcoming obstacles, leaders develop the competency they need to face adversity in the future, and their resilience has a positive effect on the resilience of their employees and on the organization.

Resilience: Tools for Change

Resiliency is more than the ability to recover quickly while navigating life's stressful and difficult times. Resiliency is developing our cognitive and emotional intelligence skills so that we can act rather than react. Building resiliency builds inner strength in us to take the moment of truth and create a healthy response to any given situation. As we build resilience, we strengthen our spirit and develop wisdom.

"It's not about being in balance, it's about how quickly we can get back to balance."

—**Rahkwees Keh,** *Native American Elder, Tuscarora Nation*

How do we get back to balance and become less stressed and more cognitively and emotionally intelligent and resilient? How do we become more conscious and self-aware so that we can relearn, rewire, and retrain our habitual habits of beliefs, thoughts, emotions, and reactions? There are 4 steps to becoming more resilient as a person and as a leader:

1. Observe
2. Accept
3. Re-decide
4. Re-wire

Step One: Observe

In yogic practices, learning to observe is often called cultivating the inner witness. When we become stressed, we become cognitively and emotionally dysregulated. This means our chatterbox of thoughts runs wild and runs all sorts of "what if" scenarios. Our mind keeps replaying the events that happened or what may happen. If we are worried, angry, upset, depressed, jealous, heart-broken, hateful, or overwhelmed, we become emotionally dysregulated and feel out of sorts. When this happens, we get caught up in our upsetting thoughts and become the emotions we are experiencing.

When we are caught up in our emotional reactions and chatterbox thinking, we run the risk of derailing our managerial and leadership effectiveness. When we are dysregulated and out of balance within ourselves, we don't have access to higher thinking, agility or creativity. We are in fight or flight mode.

We need to learn to step back, observe, witness, and accept what is happening without being caught up in the mind-stream of our thoughts and emotions. This is critical to becoming resilient. The key is to understand you are not your thoughts, you are not your beliefs, and you are not your emotions.

When we learn to step back, observe, and witness our mental chatter and how emotions feel inside our bodies, we begin to cultivate consciousness and self-awareness. We begin to open ourselves to our inner wisdom, authenticity, and our true self. Once you are in observation and witnessing, ask yourself who is it that is doing the witnessing and observing? This, oftentimes, is your deeper Self who is observing and witnessing.

To step back, reflect, and observe starts with taking a deep breath. When we become psychologically and emotionally dysregulated, our breathing patterns change. While this sounds so simple, learning to observe and take control of our breathing patterns, we recognize that stress causes us to breathe in irregular and shallow patterns. Slowing the breath down is so important.

An easy breathing pattern to intervene with the fight or flight response and cognitive and emotional dysregulation is a 4 x 4 x 4 x 4 breath, or 4-part breathing. When using this method with executives, I've witnessed them moving from a stressed, dysregulated state into a calm, balanced state in less than three minutes.

Four-part breathing means you breathe in to the count of 4, hold for a count of 4, breathe out to a count of 4, and hold the breath out to the count of 4. This totals 16 seconds. When you use 4-part breathing, you change your breathing pattern to just over 4 breaths per minute.

Just as we have ranges for blood pressure, cholesterol, weight, and heartrate, there are ranges for normal respiration. The normal respiration rate for adults is 12-20 breaths per minute. When people are stressed, we begin to breathe faster and shallower. According to yogic principles, when stressed, we generally breathe at a rate of 25-35 breaths per minute depending on the level of stress. When we are stressed, we've activated our sympathetic nervous system (SNS), our fight or flight response. When we stay in the stress response with chronic low-grade stress, we develop disease and adversely impact our health. This is because our SNS is activated. When our SNS is continually activated over long periods of time, our immune system is compromised, leading us to ill health and disease.

When we use 4-part breathing, we activate our parasympathetic nervous system, our relaxation response. I have my Apple watch programmed to remind me to do deep breathing several times per day. I've programmed what I call the 10-second breath. Breathe in for 10 seconds and breathe out for 10 seconds. Based on the way my watch works, it is very easy to take a breathing break even in the middle of a meeting. This means I am breathing at a rate of 3 breaths per minute. You will want to experiment with your breathing pattern. Some activate their PNS system at 3 breaths per minute, as I do. For others, it is 4 breaths per minute.

In my years of teaching breath-work to executives, I've noticed most people relax and activate the PNS when they breathe at an average of 5 and 7 breaths per minute. There are yogis who practice breathing only one-breath per minute. That takes a lot of practice. For now, start with observing your breath and then lengthening your inhale and exhale until you reach 5-7 breaths per minute. When I start a coaching session with a client, one of the first things I do is slow their breathing down.

As you slow down your breathing and activate your parasympathetic nervous system, you can psychologically step back inside yourself and reflect:

1. What thoughts am I having?
2. What beliefs drive these thoughts?

3. What emotions are being triggered as a result of these thoughts and beliefs?
4. Are my thoughts "the truth?"
5. Are my beliefs "the truth?"
6. Why is it so important for me to emotionally react this way?
7. Is all this true?
8. Is it really, really true?
9. What would happen if I didn't believe my thoughts and beliefs?
10. What would happen if I didn't respond emotionally the way I do?
11. How can I look at all this differently?

Step Two: Accept

Pain and suffering along with joy and happiness is the human condition. Life is full of experiences, some that you enjoy and other experiences you would rather not have. When we accept the reality of the situation, we move into acceptance.

Acceptance doesn't mean you have to like or approve of what is happening. When we are in denial of what is happening, or when we try to be strong and push through, or when we avoid and resist what is happening, we increase our stress. When we resist reality, we say things like:

1. It's not fair.
2. It shouldn't be like this.
3. They shouldn't act this way.
4. Why is this happening to me?
5. This can't be true.

No one wants to experience difficulties and pain. Yet, it happens. Accepting the reality is key to ending the emotional suffering that goes with our difficulties and pain in life. When we resist what it is, we create more emotional pain and suffering. Accepting the reality means you no longer deny reality.

Acceptance is a skill and requires practice. It means you can see the reality of the situation for what it is and accept how you are emotionally feeling about the situation. It's the ability to say, "This hurt, and I will get through it." We have numerous opportunities in life to practice acceptance. Here are some techniques to help you improve your ability to find acceptance in the most challenging moments in life:

- Accept the issue as it is. If you can solve it, solve it.
- If you can't solve it, then change your perspective of the situation. Look at the issue from two or three different angles.

When you go into acceptance, you add to your personal power, even when life is difficult.

Step Three: Redecide

From childhood, we face many difficult situations. During those tough times, we develop defensive structures designed to protect ourselves and to help us manage that moment in time. Those defensive structures, that I like to call our programs, consist of beliefs, thoughts, emotions, and behaviors.

If we are being emotionally reactive and defensive, we need to uncover those deeper beliefs and challenge the deeper beliefs that drive defensive structures. When we uncover those beliefs that cause us to derail, the next step is to re-decide and change those beliefs. Changing behaviors starts with changing beliefs. In my case, I had to redecide what it meant to be strong. My new definition of being strong meant allowing myself to accept, and feel the deep sorrow I was experiencing watching my brother-in-law slowly lose his life. It took strength to let go emotionally. To redecide, we need to reflect on our emotional reactions and the beliefs attached to those emotions. When we take a retrospective approach to viewing our defensive strategies, we begin to heal ourselves and become more resilient. This results in a more positive sense of well-being.

Step Four: Rewire the brain

When we change our beliefs and behaviors, we neurologically rewire our brain. There is a saying in neuroscience that goes, "neuron's that fire together, wire together." In 1949, Donald Hebb, a Canadian psychologist in the field of neuropsychology, made the discovery that linked behavior to cognitive thinking to neurological wiring in the brain. This means every behavior we have, both useful and non-useful ones, are wired into the neuro-circuitry of our brain. During the last 30 years, with the advent of emotional intelligence and neuroscience, business leaders now understand that to become more effective leaders, we must rewire our behaviors in the neuro-circuitry of our brain.

To start the rewiring process, you must have a deep

belief, intention, and desire to change. If you don't want to change, you won't change. You need to examine your beliefs and intentions. Saying "I *want* to change" versus "I *need* change" makes a difference in whether you will change. When you deeply desire and intend to change, even if the change is hard, your commitment will help you rewire your brain to support your change. Then, you must repeat the process over and over until the new behavior and neuro-circuitry of your brain is completely rewired.

Resilience is the foundation for the next two aspects of REAL leadership, engagement and agility. When we get caught in derailment behavior, we don't drive high engagement or collaboration. We become less agile and more inflexible. Creating a daily practice to become more self-aware by practicing self-management and self-change is the foundation for improving leadership engagement and agility.

CHAPTER 4
ENGAGING LEADERSHIP

"Trust is the glue of life. It's the most essential ingredient in effective communication. It's the foundational principle that holds all relationships."
—**Stephen R. Covey**

Stated simply, employee engagement is connection and belonging. The sense of connection and belonging occurs as a result of positive and trustful human interaction. Engaged employees need to feel an affinity with each other, their leaders, and the company. Engagement is human and emotional -- period.

Based on my years of experience with leaders, to improve their effectiveness and create high-performing cultures, the number one variable that I've witnessed that determines high levels of engagement is REAL Leadership. REAL engaging leaders know how to be human, and they foster human connection.

As discussed in the previous chapter, resilience focuses on how well leaders tap their inner resources and spiritual strength to heal and bounce back from difficult times. REAL engaging leadership is how you "show up" as a leader. Consider these questions:

1. How do you "show up" in your human interactions?
2. How well do you create a sense of belonging, affinity, and trust with your co-workers and employees?
3. How often do you take the time with your team to build relations and connection?
4. How often do you apologize for mistakes and show vulnerability?
5. Do you focus on tasks and goals and find the people side of the business too messy and too difficult to manage?
6. Do you really care about the people you work with?

When employees know they are valued, engagement increases. One of the primary ways that leaders derail, in my experience, is focusing too much on tasks, obtaining the goal at the expense of managing the employee side of the business. Too many leaders look at people as tools that can be used and discarded. REAL leaders recognize that they are part of a team and they can't accomplish anything without the support of others. No one goes it alone. Conscious leaders know how to cultivate a sense of belonging and create a trusting community, improving organizational results. Teamwork and a sense of belonging increases intrinsic motivation. This increases the commitment to collaborate and solve tough issues while enjoying the work they do.

"A leader is best when people barely know he exists,
when is work is done, his aim fulfilled, they will say,
we did it ourselves."

—Lao Tzu

During my early 20s, I worked for a lady named Cynthia. Cynthia epitomized transcendent and conscious leadership practices. It seemed innate for her to build teams and bring out the best in people. During our meetings, her first order of business was to listen to what we—her employees—had to say. Everyone would leave her meetings with a large to-do list, and excited to do it. When we made mistakes, she would mentor and coach rather than judge and critique. Within two years, every person on her team had been promoted to leadership positions. Cynthia's leadership formula was simple: help everyone succeed.

According to research at the University of Warwick, people who are happy are 12% more productive. (Drs. Oswald, Proto, Sgroi. *Happiness and Productivity.* University of Warwick. University of Chicago Press, 2015.) Another study shows that productivity improves by 20-25% when employees feel connected to the work they do and the people they work for. (Chui, Manyika, Bughin, Dobbs, et al. July 2012. Unlocking value and productivity through social technologies. *The McKinsey Global Institute*). The McKinsey study also highlighted the need for employees to be connected socially and digitally. Using technology helps employees learn, increase their knowledge, and improve their skills while helping them remain connected. The study demonstrated how social technologies can improve interaction and communication, increasing that sense of community and belonging.

REAL leaders use both the human connection and social technology to increase interaction and engagement. The human level of engagement and connection starts with how a leader actually leads. When leaders focus on the connection between people, employees become passionate about improving their productivity and hold themselves accountable for their own learning and development.

There are five qualities, characteristics, and skills that conscious leaders bring to their organizations and employees. They know how to:

1. Build trust and transparency
2. Create growth and development
3. Empower others and value differences
4. Collaborate and create alignment
5. Bring meaning and purpose to everyday life, including work life

Conscious leaders aren't perfect, but they are willing to learn and admit mistakes. They are willing to "take one for the team" and help the team move forward. Engagement doesn't mean everyone is lovey-dovey. High-engagement means creating that sense of belonging and generating a sense of safety and security for everyone on the team.

Trust and transparency

'Trust is like blood pressure. It is silent, vital to good health, and if abused can be deadly."

—**Frank Sonnenberg,** *author of Follow Your Conscience*

A foundation of trust is built on transparent communication and open dialog. As an organizational development specialist, I've learned that one of the best ways to build trust is to talk about the issues that created distrust. One of the hardest things to do is to talk about the actual issues that create distrust. When I facilitate a team session, and we talk about issues that create silos and distrust, I let them know that it takes resilience and grit to be transparent and tell the truth. These sessions are often difficult, emotional, demanding and transformational. When teams heal the issues that create distrust, a whole new energy of innovation and creativity is released.

When there is distrust, there is little transparency and a very low sense of belonging. This type of environment creates counter-productive behavior and internal competition. People lose and companies lose.

When your team trusts you as a leader, it increases their commitment to team goals. Communication improves and ideas flow more freely. When trust exists, creativity and productivity improve. In the hands of a trusted leader, employees are more comfortable with change and more willing to embrace a new vision. When your team doesn't trust you, you don't get their best effort. You'll then find yourself unable to inspire, influence, and create real change.

Transparency increases the sense of belonging. It helps people to collaborate, generate ideas, co-create, and take action together. This is what Cynthia did so well. When she invested time listening to us, we had a sense that she truly cared. She encouraged dissent and opposing views. We had tough conversations and still came out stronger as a team.

As the following study demonstrates, Cynthia created positive psychological capital because she truly cared about our emotional well-being as people.

Study: Caring managers create confidence

A 2018 study was done at the Turkish Standards Institute involving 1,200 white collar workers on the value of "positive psychological capital" created by their transformative managers.

Transformational leaders are viewed as those who affect their subordinates with charisma, motivate them toward designated goals, encourage them intellectually, and show individual interest in each of them. Transformational leaders consider the skills and capabilities just as other leaders do, but they also consider their employees' desires, needs, and values.

This caring for each individual creates "psychological capital" proportionate to the factors of hope, self-efficacy, psychological resilience, and optimism that the employees have. Transformative leaders positively affect these factors. Employees have more hope that they can reach their goals. They are more confident in their abilities, thus raising their self-efficacy. They are resilient and can readily adapt to high-impact situations. They view negative situations as temporary and are optimistic that more widespread or more permanent situations will be positive.

The study concludes that transformational leaders do

have a positive impact on the psychological capital of their employees—in all the factors studied. As a result, these employees are more likely to create innovative solutions to organizational problems, which allows the organization to become more sustainable.

As evidenced in the study, when leaders demonstrate true caring, employees increase their resilience levels, have more optimism, increase their engagement, and improve their performance. REAL leaders establish relationships with their employees. They listen, learn, and respond to what their employees say. They develop a culture of caring, respect, and trust. Employees know their ideas and feelings are valued by their supervisors and managers and feel more motivated and engaged to accomplish the organization's goals.

Extending trust and empowerment gives staff confidence to experiment. Creating a risk-taking environment is crucial in today's fast-changing digital economy. With high levels of trust, management and staff willingly and openly discuss what is going wrong as well as what is working. They seek to collaboratively find answers and move forward together to fix problems.

Growth and development

"An organization's ability to learn,
and translate that learning into action rapidly,
is the ultimate competitive advantage."
—Jack Welch

REAL leaders not only believe in growing and developing people; they champion it. They believe that if they enable and develop their people, the faster organizational results flow. REAL leaders aren't afraid to have their employees surpass them; they encourage it. In keeping with my sports analogies, coaches want each player on the team to play their best. They do that by helping them improve and build their skills. They provide the tools to do the job well. Coaches teach, challenge, and stretch athletes, helping them grow. That's what REAL leaders do in business: teach, challenge, stretch, and develop their employees, helping them grow.

Remember Chuck from Chapter 1? He was the consummate champion of people development. He recognized that the more he provided opportunities for people to grow, the better the company did. When I met Chuck in the mid-1990s, he was one of the first leaders I met who actively championed diversity at all levels of the organization. He believed in the value that differences brought to his team. As a result, he had a very diverse, highly engaged, and loyal team, and his philosophies permeated the organization.

While many organizations provide training and development, there is a difference between a leader who sends her people to the programs and then checks the box, and REAL leaders who take advantage of what the company provides and then do more. Employee growth and development is a strong indicator for employee engagement.

REAL leaders recognize that development goes beyond skill-training. Employee development encompasses knowledge-sharing, long-term development plans, and the opportunity to perform. Additionally, conscious leaders recognize that when they develop, challenge and grow their people, they build not only followers, they build future leaders. Since they are not afraid of their employees passing them, they help people achieve the highest potential. REAL leaders recognize that they will accomplish more and drive more efficient processes by trusting the smarts of their people.

An organization's long-term success is predicated on human capital. Several years ago, I worked with Patricia, the leader of an operations team in a large financial services organization. Patricia was an ex-pat. She promised her children that when it was time for them to go to college, the family would move back to the states. As her oldest entered his junior year of high school, she knew she had an 18-month window to make her transition. Moving home wasn't the issue; the issue was, who would be her successor?

Normally, this could create internal competition. But Patricia's team decided to have an honest conversation about their individual career aspirations. During a team session, we learned that five of the six people wanted Patricia's role. They realized Patricia would not be the sole decision-maker in who would replace her; there were others who would be involved with that decision. Acknowledging the reality of the situation, the team decided they would, with Patricia's help, all train and develop themselves to take her role. There would be no competition. Based on their logic and analysis, if they all prepared and developed themselves to take her role, they would all win. Only one person would get

Patricia's role, but the rest would be developed for another senior role.

They created a team learning environment and for the next 18 months – they mentored, taught, and challenged each other. This strategy helped the team with their business-as-usual jobs. The more they grew together as a team, the better they got at driving their results. Within 18 months and by the time Patricia left, two had been promoted. One was promoted to her role, and the other was promoted to lead another division. Within 24-months, four of the five senior team members were promoted.

What did Patricia do during this time? She provided resources and support to make this happen. She became the public relations arm for each of her direct reports. She looked for opportunities that could help everyone achieve their aspirational career goals. She kept them on track, delivering against business results so they wouldn't lose ground. She took the time to mentor, coach, and groom each person. She essentially became the backstop the entire team could depend on while they helped each other grow. The level of trust and transparency on this team was tremendous.

What can you do to champion growth and development? Patricia's team utilized internal training resources along with her team's talent to develop and grow each other. The hard dollar cost of that kind of mentorship and training? Zero. They would get together every Friday and have their morning coffee sessions. At first, they would meet for an hour before work. Because the meetings were so rich, their one-hour coffee sessions turned into three-hour business mentoring sessions and a once-a-month golf session. They were engaged and empowered. They created their own success strategy. The team's results doubled during that same time.

This example illustrates how investing in growth and development increases employee satisfaction and engagement. In turn, because Patricia's team had control over their growth and development, they were motivated to perform at peak levels.

Empowerment and value

> *"It's not the tools you have faith in.*
> *Tools are just tools — they work or they don't work.*
> *It's the people you have faith in or not"*
> —**Steve Jobs**

REAL, conscious leaders give power away. Empowerment means giving power away. REAL leaders aren't afraid of losing control, so they don't have to micromanage. They understand that when they empower others, more gets done, not less. Employees feel valued when they are given the responsibility, accountability, and authority to do their job.

Empowering others means stepping away and allowing them to do their own work so that they can learn, grow, and feel valued. Conscious leaders appreciate other peoples' contributions. Empowered employees are more productive and creative. They have a greater sense of autonomy and control in their work. They understand the value of what they are doing and feel like their job and role makes a difference. This increases employee satisfaction, organizational commitment, and performance.

Conversely, a lack of value and disrespect can inflict real organizational damage. Research finds that "80% of employees treated uncivilly spend significant work time ruminating on the bad behavior, and 48% deliberately reduce their effort. In addition, disrespectful treatment often spreads among coworkers and is taken out on customers" – *Harvard Business Review.*

According to research done on empowerment and organizational change, leaders need to develop new managerial skills that "maximize employee potential. These skills relate to coordination, facilitation, commitment and trust, communication, knowing more precisely what your people can and cannot do, and promoting learning and employee ownership of what they do" (Erstad, M. 1997. Empowerment and organizational change. *International Journal of Contemporary Hospitality Management*, 9(7), 325-333.) When leaders work to align teams, facilitate collaboration, and educate and inform their co-workers, high engagement is achieved, and empowerment is possible.

Many times, the reason leaders don't empower is due to belief systems that drive micromanaging and controlling behavior. These beliefs may sound like, "I can do it faster myself." "If I just tell them what to do, we can get done faster." "If I just tell them what to do and how to do it, there will be no mistakes."

1. Take a moment and identify inner beliefs you need to challenge that prevent you from giving power away.

2. Identify three new behaviors you can immediately take to give power away.

Collaboration and alignment

"It is literally true that you can succeed best and quickest by helping others to succeed."
—Napoleon Hill

Ask yourself, what is your definition of collaboration and alignment? What are your beliefs regarding the importance of collaboration and alignment? In what situation does collaborating and alignment fail? What is required for successful collaboration and alignment? Now ask yourself, how well do you drive collaboration and alignment? REAL leaders create the environment for collaboration and alignment; they don't wait for senior leadership to align at the top, although that would be nice.

I met Mike in the mid-1990s. He had just been promoted from a team leader to a director. Mike was one of the best leaders I've worked with who exemplified collaboration and alignment. He would take his own budget and set up cross-team collaboration meetings with leaders outside his team. He had three main strategies for driving collaboration:

1. Tap into the collective intelligence of his team
2. Lead cross-team collaboration sessions from his own budget
3. Demand the same collaborative behavior from his people

By the time Mike retired, he was a Senior Vice President

with 20,000 employees worldwide reporting to him. He was known for driving down costs and improving employee satisfaction through the engagement and growth of his people. He had a reputation as a great guy to work with and for. He retired at the age of 48, but after a year, he came out of retirement and took on a senior leadership role because he absolutely loved building teams, collaborating, and watching people grow and develop.

Successful leaders promote collaborative working. A recent study by the human capital research firm of i4cp found that companies that did so are five times more likely to be high-performing, achieving higher levels of productivity. Collaboration results in faster problem solving by leveraging diverse knowledge, skills, and experience. Collaboration and alignment increase efficiency and enable teams to be more strategic by valuing the different perspectives of the team members.

Senior leaders want to break down silos, drive alignment, increase engagement, and improve collaboration. Senior leaders know there is a huge opportunity lost when departments work at cross-purposes. According to surveys completed by Donald Sull, "collaboration and alignment between leaders and their direct reports are highly effective at 84%. However, collaboration and alignment between business units have an effective rate of only 59%" (Sull, Donald, Homkes, Rebecca, and Sull, Charles. March 2015. Why strategy execution unravels and what to do about it. *Harvard Business Review.*) When leaders don't cross-collaborate at the top, the lack of alignment goes all the way through the organization, adversely impacting results. This is one of the number one issues I get asked to help resolve.

What can you do to break down silos and improve collaboration? Instead of feeling like you can't do anything, do what Mike did; extend the invitation. Mike was not the CEO. He was the third or fourth level down from the C-Suite. Instead of waiting for the C-Suite to "enforce" alignment, Mike was proactive and did it himself. What one step can you take to drive cross-team collaboration?

Meaning and purpose

"Work is love made visible."
—Kahlil Gibran

REAL leaders are driven by a sense of meaning and purpose. They believe in the mission and vision of the company and align their personal mission and purpose toward the organization's goals.

Mike's deep purpose in life was to watch people grow, to move past their limitations and succeed in ways they never thought possible. Mike would align his purpose of people development with the company's vision by bringing teams together to collaborate and align. As the leader of credit card operations, he would say, "We aren't performing brain surgery. We aren't saving lives. But we are making people's lives better. So, let's be better." He would link the purpose of providing financial security and safety to the telephone banker's job. Mike would ensure that the telephone bankers knew how important their job was to their customers. He would say to them, "You are the voice and face of our company. What can I do to help you do your job better?"

In one company where Mike worked for three years, under his leadership, employee satisfaction doubled, costs were driven down 15% year on year, and customer satisfaction more than doubled. He did simple things, such as empowering employees to make decisions, rather than escalate calls to supervisors. As he drove the systemic changes of empowerment, he linked meaning and purpose to the job. Because he drove collaboration and belonging, he built a winning team, improving the bottom line and customer satisfaction.

REAL leaders continuously create and deepen meaning for their employees and their connection to the organization's vision. They interpret and reinforce the company's mission, helping contributors to see how their job fits in the organization's purpose. As a result, individuals make stronger goal commitments and report higher levels of job satisfaction.

The next generation, the Millennials, prioritize conducting meaningful work. Leaders like Mike are needed today to energize and lead the workforce. Conscious leaders are most effective when they authentically reinforce the job roles to the organization's overall purpose. Research shows that a sense of meaning matters a great deal to leaders, followers, and organizations. Positive emotions broaden existing thought patterns and help people be more creative and make better decisions.

To help drive meaning and purpose inside your organization, what messages can you send that you believe create meaning and purpose? Remember, it is not the message that you send, it is what you do as a leader, the behavior you exhibit to reinforce the message that drives meaning and purpose inside your team.

Transformational vs. transactional leaders

Another way to delineate REAL leaders from average leaders is to understand the difference between transformational and transactional leaders. Transactional leaders focus on getting the work done. Transformational leaders inspire people to reach their potential, driving increased organizational results.

According to Bass and Riggio, (Bass, B. M. and Riggio, R. E. *Transformational Leadership*, 2006), transformational leaders recognize the self-worth of others and motivate them to do more than they thought possible.

Transformational leaders set high expectations that challenge their followers and lead them to achieve higher performance. At the same time, these leaders pay attention to their followers' needs and personal development. They help their followers grow and develop into their own leadership potential.

Bass and Riggio make a distinction between transactional leadership and transformational leadership. Transactional leaders discuss what is required of followers for the successful completion of projects and specify the conditions and rewards for meeting those requirements. This kind of leader creates the environment for cooperation among leaders, colleagues, and followers.

Transformational leadership, on the other hand, raises leadership to the next level by inspiring followers to share in the leader's vision, challenging them to become innovative problem solvers. This kind of leader coaches, mentors, challenges, and supports followers, helping them to become future leaders.

What Bass and Riggio are saying is that while the transactional leader creates the environment for high performance on a case by case basis, the transformational leader creates a mindset that motivates followers to see the bigger picture and to commit to the leader's vision. The transformational leaders help employees to become more autonomous, and that enables a sustained high level of performance over an extended timeframe.

Bass and Riggio define three components of transformational leadership: *idealized influence*, *inspirational motivation*, and *intellectual stimulation*.

In their view, transformational leaders serve as role models for their followers, creating a vision that can be shared and a "collective sense of mission." The leader reassures followers that all obstacles will be overcome. This *idealized influence* comes from the leader's behavior as well as from the followers' own belief in the leader's abilities, counting on the leader to make the right decisions.

In addition to idealized influence, the authors list *inspirational motivation* as a key to transformational leadership. These leaders inspire their followers, give their work meaning, challenge them, arouse their spirits, get them enthused, and display optimism. They offer a "compelling vision of the future."

Transformational leaders also encourage creativity in their followers and offer *intellectual stimulation*. The leaders are confident in their own creativity and challenge their followers to ask questions, double-check assumptions, reframe problems, look at old situations in new ways, and change the status quo. The interchange is safe—there is no criticism allowed of any new ideas or of any member's mistakes. Leaders want their followers to look at problems and issues from many different angles.

Leaders also pay close attention to each individual follower, their strengths, and their needs. They serve as coach and mentor and look for opportunities to give their followers more opportunities and responsibilities and move them along in the organization.

Leaders recognize individual differences, holding some to stricter standards while giving others more autonomy. Leaders walk around the work areas, interacting with employees on an individual basis, having personal conversations, listening to concerns, and delegating tasks.

It is this combination of inspiration, motivation, and intellectual interaction that makes a leader charismatic and transformative.

Engagement: Tools for Change

Engagement is the commitment, passion, and the emotional connection workers have with their company and their leaders. How well leaders form deep relationships, build organizational trust, drive collaboration and alignment, challenge and develop others, and create meaning and purpose depends on their business intelligence skills and levels of resilience. If a leader, based on deeper belief structures, feels they have to micro-manage and control everything, they will drive engagement in one way. If a leader, based on deeper belief structures, is confident in their ability to empower and trust others, they will have a different style of leadership and engagement.

When people are engaged, they increase their energy, drive, and dedication to the leader and the organization. Engaged employees are emotionally committed to the leader and the organization, so they can contribute and make a positive difference. Engaged employees drive innovation, improve organizational processes, and push the organization forward. Employee engagement is low worldwide, so even a small increase in engagement can make a measurable difference. Improving engagement and emotional commitment means leaders need to change "how" they lead and "what" they do. Since engagement is an emotional connection, leaders need to look at how well they encourage and create emotional connections.

Tips to increase engagement
1. Evaluate your beliefs around empowerment, control, power, and listening.
2. Reflect and let-go of any needs to be right and the fear of failure and rewire those beliefs.
3. Actively listen: let people know they are valued.
4. Adopt others' ideas.
5. Have meetings without you: allow your teams to come up with ideas and solutions to problems, then empower them to solve the issues with their ideas.
6. Show you care: write thank you notes by hand, provide positive feedback.

7.   Publicly promote your team's accomplishments.

If, as a leader, you are unable to lead as outlined in the Tips to increase engagement, it is important that you go back and re-evaluate your resilience levels.

CHAPTER 5

LEADERSHIP AGILITY

"Learning agility means to learn, de-learn, and relearn all the time."

—**Pearl Zhu,** *Digital Agility The Rocky Road from Doing Agile to Being Agile*

To be a REAL, agile leader, you need a healthy relationship with fear. Agility means stepping outside the comfort zone and into the unknown. For most people, stepping into the unknown creates fear. Self-awareness and social-awareness skills are required to identify how fear operates within you and how fear operates around you. I can't tell you the countless times I've worked with leaders who stay in their comfort zone by confusing logic with fear. They use logic to support a point or defend a position. That only makes them sound logical and reasonable. Despite the logic, many times what drives the logic are fear-based emotions. I've witnessed leaders who make sound arguments to take action and still do not act. That's fear.

For example, Alex is the CEO of a restaurant chain. He knows he needs to change the culture. He knows he needs to modernize. He knows he needs to get his team to collaborate better and create synergies. But, because of financial reasons, he continually postpones the cultural work required to obtain the synergies he needs. He postpones the sessions where his team can and should address the deep issues that impede their effectiveness as a team. The longer he postpones for sound, logical financial reasons, the more his team continues to work in silos and against their own best interest as an organization. His fear? He is a very cautious leader, so he takes things slowly, plus he's concerned that addressing the deeper issues might bring up conflict. So, his team stays stuck, justified by logic. As a result, his team is not turning the organization around as quickly as he would like.

REAL leaders actively identify and pursue how fear shows up in their lives. They ruthlessly track down their fear-driven leadership behaviors so that they can be more discerning about the decisions they make. The more they drive out fear from within themselves, the more they can drive out fear from within the organization. REAL leaders aren't afraid of fear. They know that at the edge of the comfort zone is fear, creativity, and innovation. REAL leaders push off the comfort zone rather than being defined by it.

Being agile, flexible, and innovative means, you actively venture into the unknown. This means we have developed a powerful relationship with fear. When we leave the safety of the known and move into the unknown, we expand and grow personally and professionally. All beliefs about what it means to stay safe and to avoid risk are based on our past experiences. Why not create new experiences and new beliefs?

Being agile requires changing mindsets, beliefs, perspectives, and behaviors. My husband and I have a saying that "you can't lead people beyond where you've been." If you haven't conquered your fear of the unknown, you can't help others conquer it. If you keep yourself confined to the comfort zone, you won't be able to lead others out of it. Being a REAL, agile leader means you encourage and lead yourself and others outside the comfort zone. Whether that means speaking up when others don't agree, trying a new methodology, or creating a new product, agility is the ability to move past the discomfort of fear and into the excitement of creation.

Today's organizations are looking for flexibility, innovation, and agility. An agile organization begins with people who are agile. The opposite of being agile is being static. Static sits in the comfort zone. Agility is being comfortable with the discomfort. It is having the discipline to stay the course even when your comfort zone calls you back. It's about being confident in moving into the unknown. It is the desire to be the explorer into the unknown and the world of possibility. Agility is acting rather than reacting out of habit from our comfort zone.

To expand our comfort zone, we need to be aware of are our deep habits of thinking, believing, and feeling that keep us stuck. Beliefs are part of the unconscious mind. Uncovering our deeper beliefs that keep us tied to the known and in our comfort zone is important to creating and sustaining behavioral change. The second step of becoming agile is to change.

To change means to change your behavior. Do

something without guarantees. Take those calculated risks and then take some edgy risks. The reason organizations struggle so much with innovation and change is that it's risky. Failure might happen. There is so much fear of making mistakes inside of companies where people don't and won't change. Everyone stays put. No creativity, no innovation, and no change.

The weight-loss industry makes money on people who have great intentions to change their behaviors but don't actually make the change. In January, every year, the gyms are packed, and the numbers of people dwindle in February and March. Despite their best intentions, people don't follow through on their health plans. The comfort zone is so alluring.

> *"We are what we repeatedly do.*
> *Excellence therefore is not an act but a habit."*
> **—Will Durant.**

To become more agile, we need to look at what keeps us stuck. Every day, we are faced with different challenges. The way we respond to these challenges lets us know if we are awake and conscious or if we are operating out of habit. Expanding the comfort zone and changing beliefs is the key to creating leadership agility. You will want to question your underlying beliefs and assumptions, and ask yourself, "Am I being directly honest with myself? Am I confusing logic with my comfort zone? Do I have a fear of failing that keeps me from being agile and flexible? How agile is my team? What behaviors am I exhibiting that either drive or detract from agility?" By answering these questions, you begin to get a clue as to your agility as a leader. If we become awake and conscious, we can choose to be proactive. If we react out of habit and instinct, we operate from an unconscious base.

Remember, we are the programmers of our minds and habits. We either place ourselves in a position of choice and agility or we can stay put in our comfort zone. Even a non-choice is a choice. What we must remember is this: we are always making choices. Some lead us to create in a new way, and others lead us back down the same road of inflexibility, habit, and comfort zones. Improving agility starts with self-awareness and transcending the comfort zone. There are skills that you can build to become a more agile leader, and they are:

1. Being socially attuned
2. Building your business skills and capabilities
3. Improving your business acumen
4. Embracing change and innovation
5. Understanding the difference between discernment and decision-making

Attunement

> *"Effective leadership is not about making speeches*
> *or being liked; leadership is defined*
> *by results not attributes."*
> **—Peter F. Drucker**

Attunement is staying connected to the energetic and emotional ebbs and flow of the people around you. Sometimes, attunement is easy, like being at a concert where you can feel the excitement in the air. Or, when there is a natural disaster, and you can feel the concern and caring that people have for one another. This type of tuning in requires empathy and connection. Other times, in the midst of our busy lives, we lose our empathy and connection. We get too focused on the task that we forget the people side. We lose the human touch.

As a business leader, learning to read and manage the emotional and energetic flow of a team is a subtle skill. REAL leaders stay connected to the emotional undercurrents of their team. Having this social awareness and social intelligence opens us to our humanness. Businesses do not exist without people. How well people perform depends on how they feel working for their boss, the people around them, and what the company stands for. Without the human touch, leaders lack the skills to motivate and inspire people.

Becoming more attuned and tapping into social intelligence allows REAL leaders to get to the root cause of issues and solve them with the head and the heart. When leaders display empathy with the human touch, people feel valued and important. As depicted in the following Peter Senge quote, what type of leader are you? Are you open, curious and willing to explore what the other person has to say, or are you the kind of leader that has all the answers?

> *"Do we meet each person curious about the miracle of a human being that we are about to connect with? Or do we meet a poor person that we are about to help?"*
> —**Peter Senge,** *The Fifth Discipline.*

In Daniel Goleman's book, *Social Intelligence: The New*

Science of Human Relations (2006), he synthesizes the growing body of cultural and neuroscientific research on how we develop social awareness and manage our social relationships. Social intelligence happens between people. These relationships imply a close and empathetic human relationship that's in tune with the experiences, needs, and feelings of another person. As Goleman states, "Attunement is attention that goes beyond momentary empathy to a full, sustained presence that facilitates rapport." He further points out that, "We offer a person our total attention and listen fully. We seek to understand the other person rather than just making our own point."

When we listen and stay attuned, we move into selflessness. As a leader, when we take the time to explore and be present, we let people know they are important, we become other-centered. Listening is one of the greatest gifts a leader can give. When we listen, deeply listen, while staying attuned and connected, a whole new world of possibilities and new solutions open up. If we remain closed and stop listening, we become self-centered. The conversation and interaction become what *I* think versus what *we* think. When we stop being attuned and lose the human touch, we lose empowerment, and we lose the collective intelligence of the group

"Consider this, surveys of employees at 700 companies found they felt having a supportive boss was more important than a bigger paycheck. Caring bosses were more likely to retain employees and inspire increased productivity" (Goleman, Daryn. August 2017. Leaders who get their teams. *Korn Ferry Institute.*) This is the difference between extrinsic and intrinsic motivation. If an employee's basic financial needs are met, then intrinsic motivators become key to retaining employees and inspiring productivity. Being supportive and socially attuned to the energy and feeling of what's going on with the people inside the organization demonstrates caring.

To improve your attunement skills and develop your human touch, reach out to people and give them your time. When you give people your time, it sends the message that they are important. When people feel valued and important and feel that you care about them as a person, engagement and productivity rises.

Business skills and capabilities

> *"A leader is someone who knows the way,*
> *shows the way and goes the way."*
> —John H. Maxwell

At home, I lost the remote-control battle, so I watch more sports than I typically would if I controlled the remote. Some years ago, while watching a golf tournament with my husband, I heard the announcer say that in order to become an exceptional golfer, you had to be good at the mental game and not just the physical game. He went on to say that in the beginning, golf is 95% physical and 5% mental skill. Once you accomplish the physical skill requirements, then professional golf is 95% mental.

The announcer's comment stuck with me: that of 95% of professional golf is what happens in the mind of the athlete. Athletes know that if they want to improve their game, they must improve their physical skill. Golfers go to the driving range to practice their shots and go to the putting green to practice their putts. Basketball players go to the gym to practice dribbling and shooting hoops. Football players practice their offensive and defensive skills as well as ball handling. Additionally, athletes work on strategy. How are they going to play the game and work on teamwork? How will they interact with each other when they are on the field? Athletes have coaches who help them fine-tune their physical skills and capabilities. But coaches also help athletes fine-tune their mental game. If a player is not confident, then they won't demonstrate peak performance.

Building leadership skills requires the same discipline and practice. Business skills involve such things as strategy, knowing the numbers, project management, business knowledge, economics, and knowing the industry. Strong business leaders stay on top of their game by staying informed and actively working on these skills as needed.

Conscious leaders spend time working their mental and emotional game. This is the 5%. REAL leaders work to improve both their business skills and their leadership skills. They work on their emotional intelligence, people skills, and team skills. This requires time, discipline, and practice. Leadership is the art of getting things done through people. This may seem simple, but getting things done requires complex negotiations, conflict resolution, bargaining, and persuasion. The ethics and rationale behind what you are trying to accomplish must be considered; then, you should chart your course in collaboration with others. This requires depth of purpose, knowledge, and fortitude to operate in increasingly complex, global environments. This is the people side of business.

We've all witnessed exceptional athletes lose a game, not because they don't have the skill, but because of their individual mental and emotional states. Leaders can have all the knowledge and capability in the world. However, if you can't obtain buy-in to your vision and strategy, it will be much harder to achieve optimal performance from the people you lead. Eventually, you will derail.

As an organizational transformation consultant and an executive coach, I've met many managers who have great business skills. I've met very few people who are both gifted in business skills and have the ability to drive conscious transformation inside companies. It is a rare leader who has both of these skills and capabilities. Business skills are necessary and important. If you don't have basic business skills and capabilities, you won't go far in your career. There are exceptionally bright people out there who fail because they don't have the people skills. A REAL leader discerns what is happening, brings the right people together, and facilitates the discussions that lead to business decisions that drive performance.

Business acumen

Business acumen is one of the toughest business skills to measure and even harder to describe. Conversely, it's easy to define and measure whether someone has strategic capability, whether they know the trends of the business, or know if they are good with finances, budgets, legal concerns, or managing day-to-day operations. Business acumen is an intangible skill that, when it's missing, you feel it.

Business acumen means having the ability to understand and distinguish--astuteness. It is the ability to quickly ascertain what is happening in any given situation and know the direction that needs to be taken. Astute leaders have a keen business sense, with mental sharpness and acuity to sort out issues. They know who to pull together and how to create team collaboration to solve complex issues. They tap into the collective intelligence of a team to drive results. Those leaders with business acumen know how to balance the task-orientation side of business with the people side of the business.

Leaders who see themselves as the great savior of the company and identify themselves as the only one who can solve the issues don't have business acumen. They may have great business skills and knowledge, but they aren't tapping into the collective wisdom of the group. In time, they make the wrong decision because none of us can see all sides of the issue. Everyone has a perspective and value to bring.

You have probably witnessed this. You get a new boss, and they position themselves as coming in to "save the department or save the business" because everything is a mess. There are times when it is true there is a real mess to resolve. But you've seen these people. Every department, every business unit they go into, is a mess. The people in the positions aren't the right ones, the processes are inefficient, and the new leader is coming to the rescue.

Then there is a special type of leader who comes in and instead of denigrating all that has gone on before, sits and listens. They spend their first 60 to 90 days getting to know the division, the people and the processes. These are REAL leaders.

These leaders have the skills to facilitate powerful decisions. They create the forum for gathering differing perspectives to create high-performing teams; they facilitate healthy discussions and solutions because no one person has to have all the answers. This is business acumen.

Zenger and Folkman examined data from more than 60,000 leaders and found that leaders who were rated in the top quartile of both skills (being results-driven and building engaged teams) ranked in the 91st percentile of all leaders. Productive leaders have the business know-how and the people know-how. REAL leaders with business acumen have a unique talent to clear away roadblocks and resolve impasses that frustrate most people. They are politically astute without being politicians. They are dedicated to the goals of the business rather than personal gain.

> *"A leader has the vision and conviction that a dream*
> *can be achieved. He inspires the power*
> *and energy to get it done."*
> **—Ralph Lauren**

When I work with executive teams, I am generally asked to help them perform better together so that they can achieve their vision and mission, accomplish the strategy, and align tactically to get there. Using the sports analogy, you can have great players on a team, with great skills and capabilities, but if they can't play well together, the team doesn't work. Astute leaders have a vision of how the team works together. REAL leaders bring the team together to create the glue required for high performance.

REAL astute leaders take the time to ensure that their vision of how teams should work together is manifested in the actions, beliefs, values, and goals of leaders at every level of the organization. This vision attracts and affects every employee who is engaged in living this set of actions, beliefs, values, and goals. They want to be a part of the vision.

Change: innovation and flexibility

> *"Innovation is the difference between*
> *a leader and a follower."*
> —**Steve Jobs**

More than 70% of the senior executives in a McKinsey survey reported innovation as one of the top three drivers of growth for their companies in the next three to five years. Innovation is seen as the most important way for companies to accelerate the pace of change in today's global business environment (Barsh, Joanna, Cappazzo, Marlo M., and Davidson, Jonathan. January 2008. Leadership and innovation. *McKinsey Quarterly*).

In my consulting practice, I've often listened to leaders express how difficult it is to act outside the box. *Thinking* outside the box is easy but *acting* outside the box is much harder. When senior leaders ask me to help them improve agility and flexibility in their organizations, I ask them these fundamental questions:

1. Do you want true innovation or process improvement?
2. Are you willing to accept mistakes and missing the

mark or are flexibility and innovation only allowed if there are guarantees?

3. What is the level of risk tolerance inside the organization?

By asking these questions, I start to learn about deeper organizational beliefs that create the culture. I want to know how the leader defines innovation and change. I want to know *what's actually happening culturally* versus the value statements that hang on the walls. Aligning behavioral actions with the value statements and vision of the organization takes acumen.

I find that when I ask these questions, and the further away from the "top" I go, the more managers and leaders will say that *innovation is process improvement with no mistakes*. This is, by far, the most frequent answer I receive when I am trying to figure out why innovation is not occurring. Senior leaders will say, "Yes, we want innovation; we want change; we are willing to learn." Yet, in practice, when there is low tolerance for mistakes and failures or when people's year-end ratings suffer because they tried something and it failed, innovation and flexibility slowly die.

Part of the problem is definition. A change in process and methodology can be innovative. Then, there is innovation to develop new products or produce the next best thing since sliced bread. Innovation defined as a process of improvement is not true innovation, but it is creative and agile thinking. True innovation is drawing outside the lines.

In many ways, the answer is simple. True innovation is not happening because it is not rewarded. In fact, innovation, change, and flexibility are often met with resistance, ridicule, skepticism, and cynicism because it's outside the box thinking. Generally, the unknowns bring fear and uncertainty. With change and innovation, there is always the threat of the unknown. But going into the unknown and making change without guarantees of success is not a skill or an aptitude that is cultivated and rewarded in most businesses. The question becomes, are you excited about going into the unknown or does the unknown cause you to be cautious?

We know that focusing on innovation ensures that everyone in an organization is working toward better business practices and improving business efficiency and performance. The benefits include increased competitiveness, higher efficiency with lower costs, higher quality products, more efficient use of resources, and improved staff retention by working on challenging jobs that promote teamwork and problem-solving. Additionally, innovation creates a more proactive approach to continually match changing conditions and attract a greater number of new customers by improving existing products or offering new ones.

> *"For good ideas and true innovation, you need human interaction, conflict, argument, debate."*
> **—Margaret Heffernan**

So, how does a leader transcend the current company environment that wants to maintain the status quo? How does a leader generate change and create flexibility inside the organization? This goes back to resilience and engagement.

If I am a leader who is concerned with making goals at all cost, I can use fear and authoritative power to prod, push, cajole, and force people to get things done. If I am that type of leader, I won't get creativity out of my people.

"We cannot solve a problem by using the same kind of thinking we used when we created them."
—Albert Einstein

If I am the type of leader who wants to make goals AND get the most out of people, I will pull people together to have them generate the best ideas. Then, I will empower them to implement these ideas. An innovative and conscious leader recognizes a great idea and removes the obstacles from the path so that the idea becomes a reality. The innovative leader is not a micro-manager. They focus on the big picture and work with creative thinkers who can add to that vision to make it greater. The innovative leader needs to be able to communicate her vision and generate enthusiasm for it and needs to recognize when her project is not working and be willing to kill it, no matter how much emotional investment she has put into it.

Like innovation, leadership flexibility is a necessity in today's fast-paced, rapidly changing, globally diverse business environment. Leaders must be able to respond nimbly and with great speed in an increasingly complex world.

Discernment

"Discernment is often far more accurate than either observation or measurement."
—**Stephen Covey**

Discernment is the ability to grasp, comprehend, and evaluate clearly. Discernment helps you see beyond the facts. Discernment often comes from the gut and the intelligence to ask key questions. Conscious leaders learn to transcend the obvious facts of a given situation and look for what may be hidden in the shadows.

I once coached three executives who worked for the same company: Jack, the CEO of the holding company and conglomerate; Don the CEO of the largest business in the conglomerate; and Alan, the CEO of the second-largest business unit. Alan and Don would regularly argue over strategy, investment, and other management issues. When it was time to ask the board for investment dollars, Don had a reputation for being logical, strategic, quick to act, and stretching the truth. Alan had the reputation of being a people person, emotionally reactive, operationally driven and methodical. Jack, the CEO, was a conflict avoider, so the issues between Alan and Don grew and festered until the situation was unbearable for everyone, including all who reported to them.

Alan knew his business, but his emotional reactions made him less articulate. Don would regularly throw Alan under the bus. Alan would become defensive and react instead of using discernment to learn how to respond. Therefore, he was perceived as less strategic.

Discernment is an active capability that requires consciousness and awareness to develop. It is the active ability to discriminate what is happening with the ability to proactively and purposefully respond to a given situation.

When Alan reacted emotionally, he lost confidence. He needed to find the deeper emotional trigger to release himself from his emotional reactions and respond better. Alan needed to transcend his normal reactive patterns and become a keener observer. He needed to become astute and articulate. He needed to develop insightfulness to see beyond what Don was saying and bring forth another truth. To do this, Alan needed to improve his resilience levels, face his deeper belief structures, and change his internal triggers.

When Alan built enough self-awareness and resilience, he was able to step back and observe what Don was doing. Rather than reacting emotionally, Alan transcended his emotions and responded differently to Don's attacks. Alan could have blamed the board or his boss, Jack, for being blind and not stepping in, but Alan took personal responsibility and changed himself. This changed the interpersonal dynamics between Alan and Don. When it was Alan's turn to address the board, he was much more composed, armed with facts that ultimately changed the direction of the entire company. He learned to become discerning.

To make the right decisions, you will often have to rely on your discernment. It is the ability to see a partial picture, fill in the missing pieces intuitively, and identify the heart of the issue. If you get to the root cause of a problem, it will be easier to solve it. Effective leaders synthesize information and interpret complex or even conflicting data into meaningful action.

As Alan stopped reacting emotionally, his deeper capabilities around strategy and solving complex issues began to shine. If he reacted emotionally, the board didn't see him as ready to lead the organization. Instead of reflexively seeing or hearing what they expect, conscious leaders are strong synthesizers that recognize patterns, push through ambiguity, and seek new insights. That's what happens as you practice and develop discernment.

Risk-taking is a component of leveraging discernment. Taking risks allows you to combat stagnation and complacency. Taking risks means pushing the envelope and stepping outside of your and the organization's comfort zone. Reward and profit come in direct proportion to the risk involved. As Seth Godin, author of *All Marketers Tell Stories*, stated, "Playing it safe and not taking a risk is probably the most dangerous thing you could do in today's rapidly changing and highly competitive business environment."

As Glenda Green, an American artist and author stated, "The practice of discernment is part of higher consciousness. Discernment is not just a step up from judgment. In life's curriculum, it is the opposite of judgment. Through judgment, a man reveals what he needs to confront and learn. Through discernment, one reveals what he has mastered."

Sandra's story

Sandra was the CFO of a mid-sized, regional credit union. This was her second job out of college, and she had worked her way up through the organization. She had a great working relationship with her peers. Her boss, Walter, was retiring and wanted to promote either Sandra or her co-worker, Tom, into the role. She was satisfied with her role, and when Walter retired, she took the role of COO while Tom took the CEO role. Shortly after Walter's retirement, the board decided to do a complete audit to ensure compliance. They found a couple of minor compliance issue discrepancies but were well within regulations.

One of the board members, Phil, never wanted Sandra to be promoted. He had a business partner he wanted in the role. So, he pressed the compliance issues with the board to in an effort to get Sandra fired. Sandra only had three more years before retirement and being fired for cause would make her ineligible for her pension. Of course, Sandra, who understood that the discrepancies were well within regulatory standards, that these descrepancies were one-off issues, and that the company was fine, but the board, at Phil's urging became fearful.

Phil continued to press the issue tried to create a coup. He made a mountain out of a mole-hill. The board was divided on what to do. They spent another $10 million dollars to do a few more audits and found a few more issues along the way. These issues, although they were problems, were well within industry standards. What had been a small issue was suddenly becoming a huge issue. The more Sandra tried to explain why the board didn't need to worry about the results of the audit, the more defensive she sounded and the more argumentative she became.

Sandra's good reputation was threatened along with her

financial stability in retirement. She spent 25 years inside the organization and worked hard to create a good culture and strong leaders. It was clear to both Sandra and Tom that Phil, the board member, was manipulating the board for personal gain. What Sandra and Tom needed to do was to step back, stop emotionally reacting, and use their gut and discernment to figure out the situation. Sandra, out of fear, kept trying to prove that there was nothing wrong, which only made the board more suspicious.

Using discernment, Sandra and Tom tried a different approach. Instead of creating deck after deck showing how the policies they had in place were working, they decided to deeply listen to the concerns of each board member. This took guts because it meant they could unearth more problems. Instead of countering every issue with facts and figures, they asked questions about the greater concerns. When Sandra and Tom stopped reacting to the obvious facts of the situation and looked at the story the board members were telling themselves about those facts, they could have a conversation. This process took over a year.

Sandra was out of her comfort zone. She knew she didn't do anything wrong. Her gut told her there was an ulterior motive. She had heard rumors that Phil wanted her replaced so that he could install someone he felt was more qualified, better educated, and was a personal friend.

The more Tom and Sandra listened to the board with understanding rather than reacting, judging, and proving, they slowly won over the board. The main concern the board had was not the discrepancies. They understood that mistakes sometimes happen. They were concerned about the brand and reputation of the credit union if mistakes like these continued. As Sandra and Tom passed through each audit, the board became more confident. If Sandra had kept being defensive, trying to prove her point, she likely would have lost her job. But she used her ability to discern, to move beyond the obvious facts of the situation, and started to deal with the issues at the relationship level.

It was later learned that Phil was trying to get Sandra fired under false pretenses so that he could recommend one of his wife's friends for Sandra's role. He owed this person a favor. Subsequently, Phil was asked to leave the board. By the time it was finished, it had cost the company over $30 million dollars in audits and attorney fees when the issue could have been solved for about $1,000,000 dollars.

Sometimes, discernment means listening to your gut and backing off. Other times, discernment means having a keen sense to read between the lines of the obvious facts of the situation to see more clearly what is happening at a deeper level and to adjust accordingly. This is leadership wisdom.

Driving results

Organizational results are the by-product of people and teams performing together. Improve the way a team works together, and performance and bottom-line results improve. REAL leaders recognize that if they take care of *how* people perform together, organizational performance takes care of itself.

Agility is the amalgamation of being attuned, managing the energetic flows, bringing teams together to create, and having the acumen and discernment of knowing when to intervene.

> *"Leaders inspire accountability through their ability to accept responsibility before they place blame."*
> —**Courtney Lynch**

Employees who are given autonomy, accountability, and the freedom to do their jobs have an enormous investment in those jobs. They may make mistakes but will learn from them and will minimize or not repeat them because they relate to the job outcome in a very personal way. REAL leaders use their people skills to support people learning all along the way. REAL leaders *let people make mistakes. They teach, mentor, and coach so that learning occurs.* This is how learning agility gets baked into the organization.

> *"If you want to do a few small things right, do them yourself. If you want to do great things and make a big impact, learn to delegate."*
> —**John C. Maxwell**

Conscious leaders make developing their employees a priority. They know that if they teach, mentor, and coach, most employees rise to the occasion and make a difference and perform. Employees become creative, agile, and flexible. With increased learning, everyone becomes more efficient, and productivity and results improve.

Agility: Tools for Change

Organizational agility begins with leadership agility. Leadership agility is rooted in the belief and thinking system of the leader. If leaders fear failure and have strong perfectionistic and controlling needs, there is no agility. What leaders think and believe about staying in the comfort zone, taking calculated risks, and going outside the box determines the agility of the organization. To become more agile, you must begin by reflecting and evaluating your thinking patterns around failure, risk, innovation, and change.

To become more agile, we must be able to acknowledge where our boundaries are with failure, risk, innovation, and change, and push those boundaries if we are going to be agile leaders and drive agile organizations.

Tool #1: Evaluate personal bias, thinking and behavioral patterns

Self-awareness, understanding, and benchmarking your own tolerance for being agile, flexible, innovative, and the capability to change is the foundation becoming agile. There are many leaders who say they are flexible and innovative. However, when you dig deeper, their behaviors illustrate a strong fear of failure, the need to be right, and a tendency toward micromanagement and staying in the comfort zone. Become directly honest with yourself. Deeply evaluate how agile you really are. If you are stuck in fear-driven or comfort zoned patterns, then increasing agility starts with improving resilience. Don't get stuck in auto-pilot thinking.

Tool #2: Anticipate change

A key element of leadership agility is the ability to anticipate change. So, instead of being reactive to market changes, leaders who are agile are continually educating themselves in a very strategic way: they watch market trends, not just of their business but the economy in general. Agile leaders pay attention to and discern how political, economic, social, digital, and industry changes will impact their business. As a result, they will be able to make proactive and informed decisions rather than reactive decisions once a crisis hits or a curveball comes at them.

Tool #3: Generate new ideas and new perspectives

Agile leaders do their utmost to bring diverse people and divergent ideas together to evaluate a problem from all sides and generate creative solutions to today's complex problems. As a leader, encourage opposing perspectives, allow differing ideas, and facilitate creative solutions. You don't need to have all the answers, just bring the right people together. When you bring people together to generate new ideas and gather differing perspectives, you will increase buy-in, engagement, and passion.

Tool #4: Become a catalyst and a champion for change

Mike was one of the best leaders I have worked with. He always volunteered his division as the team to try new methodologies and change. On one hand, this was a little difficult for the team as they tried to get their day-jobs done while at the same time testing out a new system or implementing the newest training and development program. Over time, Mike's team became more adaptive when there was a crisis or a budget cut. Because they put their hand up first, Mike and his top leaders were perceived as highly competent and eventually all were promoted. Becoming a champion for change helps improve your ability to anticipate change and be more proactive.

Tool #5: Evaluate your agility skill.

Authors Joiner and Joseph (2007) published their results of a five-year study on agility. They found five different styles of agility, each with their own strengths and weaknesses.

Study: Levels of leadership agility

The subject of leadership agility was investigated by ChangeWise over a five-year period, and the results were published in *Leadership Agility* by Joiner and Joseph (2007). The study described leadership agility as the ability to step back, be reflective, refocus perspective, and take new actions based on this perspective. This describes not only the leader's ability to be agile with projects but is an overriding principle that's applied to everything the leader does.

The study involved 600 managers across a range of industries, functions, and organizational levels. The tools used in the study included questionnaires, in-depth interviews, client case studies, on-site observations, and manager journals. The study concluded that more effective leaders are more skilled in exercising four types of agility.

Agility types:

Context-setting agility refers to a leader being able to go beyond tactical or project-related initiatives to a higher level of strategic or visionary level.

Stakeholder agility refers to leaders who understand the objectives and priorities of all key stakeholders and can adjust to—and create alignment with—the views that are different from their own.

Creative agility is the ability of a leader to analyze problem situations and devise novel solutions, especially in more complex business environments.

Self-leadership agility is how capable the leader is in seeking and using feedback from others in changing behaviors to become more effective. Leaders learn from experience, ask for opinions, and take active steps to improve their performance.

In addition to *types*, the study also identified three *levels* of leadership agility: *expert*, *achiever*, and *catalyst*. It was found that these levels are reached through more effective leadership behaviors as the leader grows and develops higher cognitive and emotional capacities.

Agility levels:
The expert level of leadership describes managers who operate within silos with little emphasis on cross-functional teamwork. These managers can make incremental improvements to the organization and provide leadership in tactical matters. Their influence on the organization's overall culture and growth is minimal. They work with subordinates on projects, put out fires, and do not get involved with strategic planning.

The achiever level of leadership describes the manager who plans strategic objectives, hires the best people, and establishes the most effective processes to reach those objectives. The achiever works with stakeholders on strategic initiatives and works with cross-functional teams as needed. This level of leader does not micromanage subordinates but allows them to work together to carry out a plan and holds them accountable for the results.

The catalyst level of leadership represents the senior leader who focuses on strategic outcomes and promotes active participation, trust, collaboration, cooperation, creativity, and mutual respect. This level of leader seeks to grow personally and seeks continual feedback on how they can do better. The catalyst leader coaches team members to be better and has a positive effect on the organization, promoting harmony and encouraging a culture of cooperative innovation and sharing of ideas.

The study found that about 55% of managers were at the pre-expert and expert levels, 35% were at the achiever level, and only 10% had the cognitive and emotional abilities to make it to the catalyst level.

These ratios seem to reflect society. Most middle managers are concerned with short-range goals and tasks and live in silos where they work with a small team to accomplish single tasks. Senior leaders often understand shareholder goals and can translate those goals into organizational plans.

But there are very few catalyst-level leaders who can change the culture of an organization to the point of transforming it into a dynamic performing unit that can establish and sustain excellence over long periods of time.

An executive catalyst can lead an organization through tough times and guide it to learn from the experience and be ready for the next challenge. This kind of leader seeks feedback and encourages new ideas, promoting individual and team initiatives. The leader encourages, motivates, and incentivizes innovation. A catalyst-level leader is a REAL leader.

Just as resilience is the foundation for how leaders engage others, collaborate, and align people and teams, agility becomes the foundation of leadership wisdom. Agility means we are flexible enough to learn from our mistakes and grow beyond our limitations. In the next chapter on leadership wisdom, we will delve deeply into the qualities and characteristics of wise leadership. As Sandra and Tom learned, by moving past their fears, they engaged the board in a different way and became more agile in their approach. This allowed them to answer the deeper concerns of the board, and when those questions were answered, confidence in Sandra and Tom's leadership of the credit union soared.

CHAPTER 6

LEADERSHIP WISDOM

*"Authentic Leaders are not afraid to show emotion
and vulnerability as they share in the challenges
with their team. Developing a solid foundation of
trust with open and honest communication is
critical to authentic leadership."*

—**Farshad Asl**, *The "No Excuses" Mindset: A Life of Purpose,
Passion, and Clarity*

Leadership wisdom is the spiritual wisdom of your mind, body, and soul. It means we've let go of our needs for personal gain. Each of us, to some degree, are egocentric and driven by fear. Leading with wisdom means recognizing and letting go of fear-driven behavior and getting outside of self-driven needs to become of service to others.

Over the years, I've met many leaders who feel a lack of alignment between their true intentions and their role as a corporate executive. Wise leaders seek to be congruent within themselves. REAL wisdom means having the strength of spirit to lead from a sense of deep meaning and purpose. That sense of congruency and inner alignment is the voice within that guides us. Each of us has that voice within called your "self," "spirit," or "soul," and when we heed that voice, our behaviors and intentions align.

Wise leaders pursue authenticity, humility, selflessness and inner alignment between their beliefs, words, and actions. REAL wise leaders aren't afraid to be transparent and vulnerable. They transcend their own biases and use discernment to make good judgments. Additionally, wise leaders have the resilience to avoid being triggered into emotional reactions and have the inner strength to step back and compassionately sense, perceive, and question the nature of what is truly happening.

We can have business knowledge, facts, and emotional intelligence and still not have wisdom. Wisdom is a result of deep personal reflection. It is the inner discipline to make purposeful change based on listening to inner insight. Wisdom is the ability to weigh, discern, and synthesize facts, information, and circumstances while recognizing and embracing agreement and opposition. But we are so conditioned to react, it is difficult for many of us to step back and make wise choices. We are so patterned from our past experiences that we are unable to be clear-sighted. Many of us are blinded by our fears, biases, and judgments, and we don't even know it. How do we gain wisdom beyond our programmed selves?

Wisdom is a rare but much-needed quality in business. Leadership wisdom requires personal mastery and encompasses traits such as authenticity, transparency, compassion, and selflessness. It means working toward the greater good rather than acting from self-preservation. Wisdom takes years to develop and yet it is available every day of our lives if we choose to be directly honest with ourselves and listen to our deeper Self within.

The Serenity Prayer:
"God grant me the serenity
to accept the things I cannot change,
the courage to change the things I can,
and the wisdom to know the difference"
—Anonymous

Learning to be still is fundamental to developing wisdom. It means we've slowed ourselves down on the inside and let the chatter go. Finding stillness within requires practicing meditation and mindfulness. There are many leaders who cultivate knowledge, intelligence, and experience, but there are fewer people who develop and cultivate wisdom. To cultivate wisdom requires focused attention on developing these qualities and traits:

1. Authenticity
2. Integrity
3. Vulnerability
4. Compassion
5. Deeply-driven purpose

Authenticity

"Be yourself, everyone else is already taken."
—Oscar Wilde.

To be genuine and real is being authentic. All humans are fallible. None of us are perfect. Authentic leaders have the courage to be vulnerable and transparent. Being authentic means, we are human and vulnerable enough to admit our short-comings and do something about it.

Leaders who are transparent and whose behaviors align with their words build trust. They are honest and behave in accordance with their values. Studies find that when leaders lead with authenticity, there is a positive impact on performance. "As the results suggest that authentic leadership has a positive impact on follower performance, organizations may wish to develop their managers to be authentic leaders" (Wang, Hui, Sui, Yang, Luthans, Fred, Wang, Danny, and Wu, Yanhong. January 2014. The impact of authentic leadership on performance: role of followers' positive psychological capital and rational processes. *Management Department Faculty Publications, University of Lincoln-Nebraska*).

Remember Chuck from Chapter 2? Those who worked with Chuck described him as an amazing leader. In fact, many of his former direct reports and colleagues are still friends with him today. Chuck was known for his honesty, transparency, and directness. What you saw is what you got with him. He had no hidden agendas or pretenses. And even though he could be direct and tough, he was also compassionate, kind, and caring. As a result, Chuck engendered trust in his team and in the organizations he led. Still, he was not without his flaws. He could be stubborn and argumentative, but he was always willing to admit his mistakes, apologize, and reconsider his position.

Conversely, a former client of mine, Tim, knows he's defensive. He is triggered into defensive derailing behavior whenever someone questions his opinion. This is especially true with his female peers. If a female co-worker asks questions that Tim perceives as a challenge to his judgment, he becomes highly aggressive, verbally attacking and demeaning to her. He doesn't have the same behavioral tendencies with male co-workers.

Whereas with Chuck, when people would question his decision or judgment, he would at times become defensive, but he never shot the messenger. Furthermore, when Chuck realized he'd made a mistake, he would admit his shortcomings and start over. Tim couldn't let go and admit his mistakes. To him, it was always someone else's fault.

> *"Personal mastery is the discipline of continually clarifying and deepening our personal vision, of focusing our energies, of developing patience, and of seeing reality objectively. As such, it is an essential cornerstone of the learning organization—the learning organization's spiritual foundation."*
> —**Peter M. Senge,** *The Fifth Discipline: The Art & Practice of The Learning Organization*

Being genuine and authentic means your actions, motives, feelings, and words are aligned. In other words, you are in total alignment with your intentions, behaviors, and actions. While Tim is aware of his pattern and wants to change, he also says things like, "Well, that's just the way I am." Tim lets himself off the hook because he doesn't want to change. If Tim truly wants to change, he must transcend his own definition of himself. It is difficult to transcend our self-definitions. As we discussed in Chapter 3 on resilience, we are in love with our behavioral patterns, even if they don't serve us anymore. Tim loves his comfort zone of defensiveness more than he loves the possibility of making real behavioral change.

Wise leadership requires integrity aligned with authenticity. If you believe you are wrong, say so and correct the behavior. Align your words and actions with how you now feel. Realize what you have been doing wrong, be open about it, and tell people you are working on it. In Tim's case, he's slowing learning to admits his mistakes. Changing his behavior is proving to be difficult for him. In Chuck's case, he is aware, takes responsibility, and implements changes. He continually develops personal mastery over his habits and programmed behavior. Chuck acts; Tim merely tries. This is the difference between an average leader and a conscious leader.

Studies show that when leaders are authentic and their behaviors are in alignment, organizational performance increases. In today's climate, integrity and honesty are essential to building solid cultures. Authenticity and behavioral integrity increase emotional and affective connection and bonds between people.

Authentic leadership has been demonstrated to drive follower effective organizational commitment, performance, and organizational citizenship behaviors through trust in the leader and identification with the leader (Walumbwa et al. 2008, 2010, 2011).

Similarly, *behavioral integrity* has been demonstrated to drive follower performance and organizational citizenship behaviors through perceived trust in and satisfaction with the leader and follower affective organizational commitment

(Dineen et al. 2006; Palanski and Yammarino 2011; Simons et al. 2007).

Another study on authentic versus transformative leadership shows that authenticity is the foundation to becoming a transformational and transcendent leader.

Study: Authentic vs. transformational leadership

In *Ethical Leadership: A Review and Future Directions*, Michael E. Brown and Linda K. Trevino compare the similarities and differences between authentic and transformational leadership. Both types of leadership share altruism (a concern for others). Both demonstrate ethical leadership, and both show moral judgment. However, there are some key differences.

Authentic leadership

Authentic leaders are self-aware, transparent, confident, recognize their own values and moral perspectives as well as those of others, are resilient, optimistic, engaging, and high on moral character.

Authentic leaders view ambiguous ethical issues from a variety of different perspectives and can make decisions that align with their own moral values. In addition to being aware of their own self-interests, they are also motivated by end values and concerns for others.

Authentic leaders follow their own morality, are open to discussion, accept opinions, encourage interaction, and make decisions confidently. They create an environment where others can offer ideas safely and with a sense of real contributions.

Transformational leadership

Transformational leadership takes things a step further by changing the commitment and motivational levels of others to make the environment more dynamic. Some researchers suggest that transformational leadership influences others by inspiring them to look beyond self-interest and work together for the common good. Other researchers say it all depends on the motivation of the leader, who could be ethical or unethical. Transformational leaders, then, could be real or pseudo leaders.

Real transformational leaders have legitimate moral values, such as honesty and fairness, and practice management versus manipulation. Pseudo-transformational leaders are more politically motivated and have selfish principles, encouraging others to act in accordance with the leader's motives.

Subordinates look up to real leaders who have high moral reasoning, high integrity, and an acute sense of ethics. Transformational leaders care about others, consider the ethical consequences of their decisions, are consistently aligned with their own morality, and are ethical role models. They are personal and charismatic in influencing those who follow them.

Transformational leaders provide visionary and intellectually stimulating leadership as well as hold followers accountable for ethical standards through rewards and disciplines on a transactional basis.

Authentic, transformational leaders have the charisma to generate followership. They create cultures of transparency. They align people toward the common good. Authentic, transformational leaders have high ethics and moral standards. They have a brand of transparent dealings. Most importantly, their behaviors are aligned with their words.

This study, along with all the research mentioned within it, supports the idea of REAL Leadership, where leaders are recognized as resilient, engaged, agile, and possess the leadership wisdom that enables them to transform cultures, build aligned teams, and increase organizational performance.

Authenticity is a requirement for a REAL leader. It is important for the leader's health as well as his or her effectiveness on the job. When employees see authenticity in their leaders, they are attracted to it. When a leader acknowledges the feelings and values of everyone in the organization, they respond with a greater sense of commitment. Authenticity is "being real" in a way that a leader can be comfortable with the decisions he or she makes because those decisions "feel right." REAL leaders encourage authenticity in their organizations so that everyone feels confident in expressing their own true feelings and opinions without personal judgment. These organizations are healthier, happier, more aligned with management, and more successful.

Integrity

"Honesty is making your words conform to reality.
Integrity is making reality conform to your words."
—**Stephen Covey**

Integrity comes from the Latin root, *integras*, which means *soundness, wholeness, completeness.* (*Wikipedia, The Free Encyclopedia*). Integrity is a state of being whole and adhering to moral and ethical principles. (*Dictionary.com*) When REAL leaders have integrity, their words and behaviors are aligned. There are many people who say one thing and do another. The best leaders are those who are congruent between what they think, believe, say, and do

During a team session with a financial services company, it became clear that one member of the team was immensely difficult to work with. Ron was considered charismatic, smart, manipulative, and out for himself. In team sessions, he would publicly agree with the decisions, but privately, he would undermine the decisions if he didn't agree with them. Ron was someone you wanted to have a beer with but not someone you would want to work with.

During the team session, he was given feedback on his lack of integrity. His peers didn't trust him to follow through, nor did they trust him to have their back. His reputation was that he was out for himself and didn't care about others. The only time he appeared to care about others on the team was when he wanted something.

It's amazing how much devastation the lack of integrity has on teamwork, productivity, and organizational results. When people don't trust someone on their team, the amount of energy spent on work-arounds and "covering one's you-know-what" is enormous. Instead of having open and honest dialog, debates, discussions, and creating an aligned strategy, people end up working in silos and, therefore, against each other.

REAL leaders have integrity, a state of wholeness, and adhere to high moral and ethical standards. Wholeness is the sense of oneness, unity, totality, and completeness. Aligning beliefs, thoughts, inner motives, and drivers with behavior creates that sense of inner oneness and wholeness. Frequently, you see the lack of integrity and wholeness in politics, where politicians will say one thing in public and then, votes completely opposite of what they say. Organizational politics is the same. With Ron, he was seen as a political animal saying one thing and doing another.

Although Ron received feedback about his behavior, his strong need to be right led him to believe his own press. He couldn't take the feedback. He convinced himself that his teammates were incompetent, so he "had to" drive and push hard to get people to follow his lead. This is classic derailment as discussed in Chapter 2. Eventually, Ron's behavior caught up with him. He had pissed off enough people that eventually, there was no one left to support him. He left the organization never quite understanding what happened, feeling victimized, and never owned up to how his lack of integrity played an important role in his downfall.

To be complete and whole, peel back the layers of your onion and reflect on when you have been in alignment. How does it feel? Deeply reflect when you have not been in alignment between your deeper beliefs, thoughts, speech, and actions. How does that feel? Having led hundreds of leadership workshops and coached thousands, what my clients tell me is that when they act in alignment with their internal deeper beliefs and thoughts, even when the situation is difficult, they build self-confidence and self-esteem. Clients also share with me that when they don't act with integrity, they regret it. As John Wooden states, "The true test of a man's character is what he does when no one is looking" (former UCLA coach and author of *The Pyramid of Success*).

This leads us to why moral character is an important component of integrity. There have been plenty of world leaders who have gotten into their roles who didn't have moral character. Such examples include Napoleon, Stalin, Saddam Hussein, and others. They espoused one set of beliefs, but really, they were only concerned about their power and wealth. Moral character is deeply understanding the difference between ethical and non-ethical behavior.

Recently, I had a conversation with Thomas, the CEO of a large bank. He was looking to prevent fraud, especially in the wake of what happened at Wells Fargo, where some of the most unlikely people opened non-existing accounts to improve their performance. The more we talked, the more he shared his views on ethics. He went on to say that some of his neighbors, who are quite wealthy people, would often talk about fraudulent ways to avoid paying taxes. He was appalled by these conversations.

First, he knew his neighbors were wealthy enough to pay the government taxes, but then, to openly conspire with each other on how to beat the system, made him very uncomfortable. He recognized that part of what his neighbors were doing was part of a cultural belief that it was okay to cheat the government out of taxes but wrong to lie to one's friends. His ethics said defrauding the government was equal to—and the same as—dishonesty with one's friends. Thomas is an example of someone who lives and breathes integrity. Integrity is doing the right thing even when no one is looking.

Vulnerability

Leadership vulnerability is an asset. Vulnerability takes courage and strength. Some believe that being vulnerable means exposing one's weakness, therefore leaving you open to being attacked. The etymology of vulnerability comes from the Latin root *vulnerare*, which means to wound, hurt, injure, and attack. But being vulnerable also means to be open and to express oneself emotionally, authentically, and truthfully. When leaders are vulnerable and human, they engender trust. Vulnerability allows people to relate and connect to one another. This is a leadership skill, not a weakness. When people on teams and in organizations trust each other, they create the foundation for high performance.

Inner strength and self-esteem are required for vulnerability. Everyone has their moment of weakness and insecurity; that is what makes us human. What makes us REAL leaders is creating that level of connection that says, "I understand. I feel that way too, at times." Leadership vulnerability is more than openly admitting our shortcomings and fears; it also means sharing how they feel and what they do during those times of momentary weakness. This type of deep sharing is what brings people closer together and strengthens the bond between them.

It's that poignant movie scene in *The Lord of the Rings: The Two Towers* when there appears to be no hope. It is in that moment during the Battle of Helms Deep, when Aragorn sees the fear in everyone's eyes, rises to the occasion, admits his fear, and everyone rallies together to overcome the situation. Three hundred men against 10,000 orcs. At this point in the movie, everyone is tense, anxious, and fearful of what lies ahead. The music is deep, dramatic, and hypnotic, drawing the audience deeper into anticipation of what will happen next. Aragorn shares his fear with Legolas (the elf) and then, bravely rallies his courage to face the enemy. Later in the scene, as they are going into battle, Legolas says, "Your friends are with you, Aragorn."

Vulnerability pulls people together. Stepping out of the comfort zone, naming it, facing emotional difficulties and using courage inspires others to take action and to make changes. Our ability to be transparent and vulnerable with our people creates strong bonds. This leads to stronger engagement as everyone pulls together.

Compassion

Compassion is the ability to deeply care for the welfare of others. The etymology of compassion is from the Latin root *com,* meaning *with* or *co* and *passion*. Literally translated, *compassion* means *co-suffering*. Compassion is the innate desire to alleviate another person's suffering. When we are compassionate, we let go of our own needs and become selfless. This is an important distinction with transcendent leaders.

Good leaders are caring, kind, and empathic. I've seen many friendly leaders who lose compassion when they sense potential failure or when they think something may go off the rails. Under stressful circumstances, even good leaders will start to make fear-based decisions. Fear-based decisions are all about "one's self" and avoiding failure. Compassionate leaders create the cultural environment that allows people to become more creative, driving results even when difficulties arise. Problem-solving and creativity bring together the community, where everyone's "self" is included.

Is compassion inborn or learned? Is compassion intrinsically motivated or are we compassionate because we will get a reward? According to the latest scientific research, compassion is innate. We are born with compassion. We learn how to be heartless.

We see compassion in children and in babies. When children see other children hurt, they have an innate desire to 1) look and pay attention, and 2) go to help. How many times have you seen children, perhaps even your own children, reach out and comfort another child?

There are studies now that show how compassion is genetic and perhaps linked to the survival of the human species. Compassion may have ensured our survival because of its tremendous benefits for both physical and mental health and overall well-being. This idea is supported by research done by APS William James Fellow Ed Diener, a leading researcher in positive psychology, and APS James McKeen Cattell Fellow Martin Seligman, a pioneer of the psychology of happiness and human flourishing. The research suggests that connecting with others in a meaningful way helps us enjoy better mental and physical health and speeds up recovery from disease.

"Furthermore, research by Stephanie Brown at Stony Brook University and Sara Konrath at the University of Michigan has shown that compassion may even lengthen our life spans" (Seppaia).

As a result of life experience, we sometimes lose our compassion and can become cynical and self-centered. When we go through enough difficult times, we can develop an attitude of not caring. This happens when we let go of our connection to others. When we do this, as leaders, we miss a lot of information about what is going on around us. If we are not compassionate and connected, or if we think people are too emotional or hyper-sensitive, we miss important clues as to what is happening in the culture and our surrounding environment. We lose our capability to be socially attuned.

Compassionate leaders are distinctly connected to those around them. Monica Worline and Jane Dutton, authors of *Awakening Compassion at Work*, describe two different ways that compassion manifests itself in leadership practices. They describe "leading for compassion" as actions that leaders take when they use their position or personal influence to direct organizational resources that alleviate suffering. For example, when leaders sanction paid time off for employees to help volunteer for disaster relief projects, they are leading with compassion.

Study: Compassion requires resilience

Research has shown that women tend to have a better awareness of others' emotions and needs than men and have a deeper perception of the suffering of others—along with the desire to help in some way. Effective leaders have a self-awareness that enables them to be a positive influence in difficult situations.

In a study of 46 participants conducted by Fernanda Pires and others, it was found that effective female leaders who understood their own needs and limits and had a good sense of self-compassion, meaning they were resilient and gentle on themselves, realizing that their own faults were part of a larger human experience. They had a more positive view of the world.

Several measurements were used in the study, including a Self-Compassion Scale (SCS), Perceived Stress Scale (PSS), the Beck Depression Inventory (BDI), and the Mindful Attention Awareness Scale (MAAS).

The study concluded that people who are aware of the needs of others and can aid and support without experiencing stress themselves are more likely to be effective when disruptive changes occur to the organization or to individuals in that organization. This is especially true for leaders and people in more stressful occupations, such as health care.

Once again, this study supports the premise that the starting point of becoming a REAL and conscious leader starts with resilience, self-awareness, and self-regulation. To become compassionate and tap into our innate capabilities for compassion, we must overcome fear-driven and non-caring behaviors and attitudes.

Purpose-Driven

Being purpose-driven is a deep, driving force, and your reason for being. Purpose is what gives meaning to your life. Having a clearly defined purpose helps you create your personal and leadership roadmap.

You may ask, "How can I tell the difference between obsessively driven behavior and purposefully driven behavior?" Sometimes, it is difficult to tell them apart.

Purpose releases energy. The higher the purpose, the greater the energy. Purpose frees us. The more profound the purpose, the greater the sense of freedom. Purpose opens possibilities. Obsessive behavior is a result of the fear of failure. Purpose allows flexibility and agility. Obsession is single-minded and controlling.

"Obsession drains our energy and binds us to the activity itself. Less joy, less energy, and less freedom are the results. When observing the passionate, focused behavior of people, it can sometimes be difficult to know if they were being passionately obsessive or passionately purposeful. If the behavior is adding energy, joy and fulfillment to them and others, then it is probably coming from a purposeful place" (K. Cashman, *Success: 8 Principles of Purpose-Driven Leadership*).

Living with a sense of purpose is about creating; it is about evolution and forward-thinking. When you are purpose-driven, you know it is important to step away to gain a broader perspective. When we step away, we allow new ideas to generate. Those who live with a sense of purpose and who want to make a difference are happier, more content, and at peace.

Living with a sense of purpose can mean being the most loving and caring parent to your children. Or it can mean changing people's lives in another sense, such as Blake Mycoskie, the founder and owner of Tom's Shoes. He developed the One-for-One campaign. His business model helps a person in need whenever someone purchases a product from his business. When a customer purchases one pair of shoes, another pair is given to a child in need. This One-for-One idea began during his travels. "TOMS humble beginnings happened unintentionally. While traveling in Argentina in 2006, Blake witnessed the hardships faced by children growing up without shoes. His solution to the problem was simple, yet revolutionary: to create a for-profit business that was sustainable and not reliant on donations. Blake's vision soon turned into the simple business idea that provided the powerful foundation for TOMS" (Excerpt from TOMS website).

Most business schools teach that the purpose of business is to maximize shareholder value. The tide is changing. More organizations are recognizing the need to add social responsibility to that equation. Mycoskie's vision for his company grew out of his compassion and heart for children he saw in need. Since starting TOMS, his business has delivered over 86 million pairs of shoes along with restoring sight with eyewear for 600,000 people and has provided 600,000 weeks of safe water since 2014.

Your perceived purpose might not be as lofty as Mycoskie's, so you will want to find a purpose that fulfills your heart and brings meaning into your life. Finding what your purpose is drives passion and leadership. Those who live with a purpose ensure that it happens. When this happens, wisdom comes.

Wisdom

"If your actions inspire others to dream more, learn more, do more, and become more, you are a leader."
—John Quincy Adams

What does it mean to be a wise leader? Wise leadership is the intrinsic ability to discern, discriminate, and then, decide. Leading with wisdom means having sound judgment based on discernment. Wise leaders are teachers. They are no longer driven by self-interest, ego, and fear; they are driven by what brings the greater good not only for today but for the future.

How do we cultivate wisdom? Mike Thompson, Professor of Management Practice and Director of the Centre for Leadership and Responsibility at the China Europe International Business School, and CEO of Goodbrand, conducted a study on wisdom working with 88 executives in Western countries and 94 Chinese executives of commercial industries. According to Thompson, wise leaders:

1. Have foresight;
2. Use reason, experience, and careful observation;
3. Allow for non-rational and subjective elements

when making decisions; and,

4. Have an orientation beyond self-interest and towards the Common Good.

In the REAL model of leadership, wisdom includes the ability to create an inspirational vision and using discernment to make decisions (agility). Wise leaders are socially attuned and weigh both people and process data to make good decisions (engagement), and they lead with authenticity, compassion, and integrity for the common good. Wise leaders are aware of their judgmentalism, biases, derailers, and social programming (resilience) and rise above those qualities and characteristics. They are honest and self-aware enough with themselves that they can then practice agility and make fundamental changes in their behaviors. Wisdom is acquired by the accumulation of life experiences, with one distinction: wise leaders fail, learn, and start over. They apply the wisdom gained from life experiences to continue their personal and professional development.

Using compassion with a sense of purpose, a conscious leader can authentically engage their followers who share the same goals, challenges, and accomplishments. REAL leaders create a learning environment where people trust and help each other. The leader supports as well as leads. This leads to high-performing cultures and organizations.

Leadership Wisdom: Tools for Change

Leading with wisdom means becoming conscious and aware. REAL Leadership wisdom is the *how* of leadership and how you are as a person. Leading with wisdom means using our deeper, inner wisdom as a guide for our behavior and our thinking. Wisdom is acquired and learned over time. It is developed as a result of reflection and being humble enough to learn from our mistakes. Being wise means we are willing to question our beliefs and biases to change and shift our personal mindset. A wise leader, like most leaders, fail and makes mistakes, but wise leaders have the courage to admit their mistakes and failures, are accountable and responsible, and learn and change.

"Knowing yourself is the beginning of all wisdom."

—Aristotle

To develop deeper wisdom

1. Be more open-minded. Be open-minded to others' perspectives, ideas, and views and allowing their views to influence your ways of feeling and thinking. When you are open-minded, you can see a larger picture than when you are only open to your own ways of thinking and believing. This means having emotional and intellectual humility to admit that your way is not "the only way."

2. Be directly honest. While there is information that must be kept confidential, being directly honest with yourself and with your co-workers is an important quality. Direct honesty means not only sharing the "what" is going on when you can but allowing people to honestly see how you feel emotionally. Don't lie. If what you must do is difficult, say so. Let people "see you" emotionally.

That doesn't mean crying and yelling but allowing others to see your heart and humanity.

3. Show genuine interest in others. When people know you truly care about their well-being as people and as co-workers, those people will support you. Most people want to know they matter as people and that what they have to say and share matters. Show people they matter to you.

4. Go outside your comfort zone: Expose yourself to new experiences, new challenges, and new ways of thinking. Try new things. Allow others to try out their ideas when solving problems at work and coach them.

5. Ensure your decisions are based on what is best for the greater good for all concerned and not fulfilling a personal need or avoiding some internal fear. Wise leaders act in the best interest for the greater good for all concerned. They are self-less. They have checked their ego.

CHAPTER 7

TRANSCENDENT LEADERSHIP & MINDFULNESS

"Your mind is your instrument.
Learn to be its master and not its slave."
—**Remez Sasson,** *author of Will Power and Self Discipline*

REAL leaders know who they are. They know there is a deeper sense of self, spirit, and soul versus the conditioned self. It means they've learned how to transcend their conditioned responses and programs based on personal history. Being a REAL transcendent leader means having a spiritual awakening to the expansive capacity of heart-driven leadership.

Many leaders are gifted and talented with business skills and acumen. They know how to drive results and influence others. These talented leaders are good at strategy and decision-making. But that doesn't mean they are wise and transcendent leaders.

A transcendent leader brings a special quality of energy, passion, and spirit to the teams they lead. They recognize that leadership is also about managing the energy flows and passion of the people in the organization. Transcendent leaders can best be described as servant leaders who listen, sense the environment, and feel. When employees know their leader has their back, they will go out of their way to make sure the leader is successful.

The business of leadership includes strategy, methodology, processes, efficiencies, and results. The heart of leadership means we have the courage—with *"cour"* meaning *heart*—to be authentic and human. It also means we use our head to find the best way to implement what is needed while leading others.

In his book, *Spiritual Leadership*, J. Oswald Sanders quotes R. E. Thompson's definition of spiritual and transcendent leadership:

1. Do you use other people's failures to annoy or challenge you?
2. Do you "use" people, or cultivate people?
3. Do you direct people, or develop people?
4. Do you criticize or encourage?

When people are inspired, they naturally create and perform and drive results. To be inspired means to be "in-spirit" and to be connected to the divine inner wisdom and guidance that we all have access to. This feeling of being "in-spirit" releases energy and creativity. We awaken to the deeper Self within us. We acknowledge that there is something greater than us. We can it call it our deeper, wiser self that is beyond the programming, our True North, our universal consciousness, or we can call it God. When we are inspired and "in-spirit," we wake up and align our hearts and our heads.

Over the last 29 years, I have worked with many leaders, and I can count on one hand those I define as truly exceptional, REAL, and transcendent leaders. The key differences come from what drives them and their inner motives.

A client and friend of mine, Mark, is an amazing example of a transcendent leader. When his people spoke about him, they described Mark as humble, compassionate, and authentic. They said he was willing to admit when he was wrong or out-of-line, willing to listen, and willing to be selfless. Mark recognized that he didn't have all the answers and relied on the intelligence of his people to help make the best decision. His people felt supported and inspired to do their best work. Not only was Mark a great guy to work for, but he had all the business skills needed, including industry knowledge, project management, strategic skills, and good judgment. He focused on the growth and development of his people, which led them to feel challenged. These are all the components of REAL leadership. Mark, although he would not say this about himself, is a wise and transcendent leader.

When we lead from the heart, we become selfless. I want to differentiate between leading from the emotional heart and leading from a wise heart. Many people confuse the two. An emotional heart means we are leading from either the emotions of the moment or from our past. It means we lead from our personal history and, therefore, our unconscious self. Leading with an emotional heart means we are leading from fear or comfort—our flight or fight response.

Leading from a wise heart means we recognize and *feel*

our emotions, but we don't *act* from those emotions. We act from a deeper sense of purpose, authenticity, and service. Sometimes, the strongest act from the wisest heart is the compassionate, painful firing of someone.

Consider the differences between management/ leadership and transcendent leadership:

Management/Leadership	Transcendent Leadership
Mission and Vision	Purpose
Strategy	Movement: Business as a Force for Good
Goals and Objectives	Purposeful Action
Methodology and Process	Creative Agility
Competition	Cooperation/Alignment
Directive: Get Things Done	Supportive
People Leader	Servant Leader
Encouraging	Inspiring
Executive Presence	Being
Head	Heart
Thinking	Awakened
Ambition	Selfless: Greater Good

On the one hand, leadership is about driving performance and results. But a key to increase performance has to do with the "how" of leadership. Defining the strategy, goals, and the tasks is easy. Whereas, aligning the behavior of people is possibly the hardest task of leadership.

Leadership is not just about pulling people together and creating more efficient processes; it's about engaging the hearts and minds of people toward a common cause to achieve a greater purpose. This means awakening the hearts and minds of people. This is the spirit of REAL leadership.

Mindfulness and the heart of leadership

The heart of leadership means leading with feeling, compassion, transparency, and authenticity, combined with the wisdom of experience and knowledge. The strongest leaders are inspirational while driving performance. They maintain the broader perspective while managing a significant amount of complexity and detail. Leaders understand their business and create efficient processes while remaining open to (and excited about) challenges, as well as spurring innovation and continuous improvement. Leaders need to develop and empower people while avoiding costly mistakes. This requires the wisdom of knowledge, deep insight, and resilience.

Amazingly, mindful meditation, as a practice, is one of the best ways to develop these leadership traits. It is not difficult, but it does require consistency.

As leaders, our day is filled with constant distractions. Our inbox fills up with hundreds of emails, all requiring our attention. There are mini-crises (or perceived crises) that sometimes demand immediate solutions. The ability of leaders to slow themselves down on the inside is critical in order to gain mental clarity, perspective, and focus, all of which are paramount to good decision-making.

A 2017 study of leaders conducted by author Michael

Chaskalson, CEO of Mindfulness Works, Ltd., showed that training executives in an 8-week Mindfulness-Based-Stress-Reduction (MBSR) program and teaching mindfulness techniques helped executives improve in the areas of empathy, focus, perspective, emotional regulation, and adaptability. Mindfulness training has proven to be effective in leadership development.

REAL leaders and spiritual strength

Today, there are many studies being conducted on spirituality in the workplace as a core strength for highly functioning executives and organizations. Spirituality in the workplace can have a profound effect on the effectiveness of personal leadership, strategic leadership, and team leadership.

What makes leaders better is their sense of ethics and their ability to engage followers in acquiring similar attitudes and values (personal, team, and organizational) and accomplishing similar goals.

Transcendent leaders have a core value of humility, morality, and altruistic love. REAL leaders are attuned to spiritual values they practice every day in some way. Practicing spiritual values may involve prayer, meditation, yoga, and going into stillness. This helps the transcendent leader develop the inner resources and spiritual strength to continually cultivate a service mentality and mutual trust and respect.

In his book, *The 7 Habits of Highly Effective People* and *Principle-Centered Leadership*, Steven Covey discusses leaders serving others while maintaining balance and harmony in the face of constant change and external pressures. He expresses the successful habits of constant learning, believing in others, honoring value, exuding positive energy, facing life as an adventure, and leading balanced lives.

Covey's four principles of leadership include personal trustworthiness, interpersonal trust, managerial empowerment, and organizational alignment. Leaders begin with inner practice, developing themselves, and then, move outwardly toward interpersonal, managerial, and organizational levels.

Shuniya: spiritual awakening

In Kundalini Yoga, Shuniya is the state of "no-thingness." In order words, Shuniya is a zero state. In Shuniya, we move beyond our habits and patterns and move into transcendent consciousness. We move from a definition of personality and ego to expansiveness and nothingness. Shuniya means to let go. We let go of our self-identity, the "I am," and expand our awareness and consciousness until we are simultaneously nothing and everything at the same time.

Normally, we live in the world of identification, the "I am." We say, "I am smart. I am strategic. I am not sensitive. I am hyper. I am an extrovert. I am an introvert. I am driven. I am logical. I am sensitive." The list goes on. We have been defining ourselves our entire lives. These "I am" statements are the programs and beliefs of our consciousness and subconscious. These programmed beliefs become the foundation of our behaviors, both useful and non-useful.

Sunyata (*Shuniya*) is a Sanskrit word used by Brahmans for emptiness or "devoidance," and it derives from the root meaning *hollow*. It is related to the early Buddhism term *anatta* and refers to a positive emptiness where there is no sense of time, no beginning or end, a stillness of the mind—a zero state.

When we go into a deep state of meditation and still the mind, we can experience the sense of no-thingness, Shuniya, no time and no place. In this state, we've moved beyond "I am" into a more expansive and transcendent state. In the state of Shuniya, we let go of fear. In fact, it is impossible to experience fear in the state of Shuniya. We let go of our programmed beliefs and go beyond the beyond and see life and the situations in life differently.

The Brahman concept is one of empty space but also a feeling of fullness. There is no sense of individuality but only connectedness—everything is interdependent. Individuals who reached this zero-state have a sense of the greater good and feel loving and caring toward all others. This concept of universal caring is important for all leaders because it is fundamental to their success in cultivating teamwork and harmony in their companies.

When I work with executives and teach them how to achieve these states of consciousness, it is amazing to watch what happens when I lead them into problem-solving from that state. When I begin a coaching session with a client, I first listen and ask questions about the issues the leader is struggling with. Many of my clients are in senior leadership roles inside of Fortune 500 companies. Generally speaking, their questions have to do with the interpersonal dynamics between people that adversely impact organizational performance.

Many times, I will take my client into deep introspection and mindful meditation. When I know they have transcended their normal monkey-mind consciousness, I then lead them through meditative problem-solving. The level of creativity and innovation that occurs while in that state of consciousness is amazing. You can't solve your problem with the same consciousness that created the problem.

Becoming spiritually awake is an expansion of self, soul, or spirit. As we reach no-thingness, our identity opens and expands outward and encompasses wider realities. When we learn to reach the state of Shuniya, we have reached that expanded sense of Self.

This is the Self within, your deeper, wiser Self that is connected and expansive and yet, at the same time, can focus on the here and now. In this state, we can move beyond our programmed self and see things in a whole new way.

The transformative process

> *"No problem can be solved with the same level consciousness that created it."*
> —Albert Einstein

Father Tom Keating, a Trappist Monk, says that "bringing oneself to nothingness is the first step in the transformative process. We must allow ourselves to be unconditionally loved and inspired to meet the real needs of the human family, past, present, and the time to come."

Hinduism teaches that the self (*atman*, soul) exists in permanence. But Buddhism believes that there is no such permanent, unchanging self. The teachings of no-thingness, non-attachment, and Shuniya are all similar concepts. In order to change, you transcend your current self-definition to a more experiential feeling where we feel connected, whole, and expansive, where self-definition disappears and you feel one with the universe.

An increasing number of scientists are beginning to agree with Buddhists that cognitive facilities are not fixed but can be trained through meditation. Meditation helps individuals train the mind. Many of us have chatterbox minds that run wild with all our fears, concerns, hurts, anger, pain, and so on. When we meditate, we learn to control the chatterbox mind and learn how to take control of the aspects of our brains that are wired for fear. When we do this, we develop deep, inner self-empowerment.

Traditional neuroscience holds that we cannot control our autonomic nervous system. However, this view is changing. Based on studies with Buddhists monks, scientists are now finding evidence that through meditation, you can control your heart rate, lower your blood pressure, and silence the fear-based voices in the mind.

In yogic traditions and eastern practices, people believe that the self-definition is an illusion. The self-definition illusion that we label as "I am" is created by life-defining experiences we had in our past. From those life-defining moments, we create our self-identity. To change our self-definition, we replace our defensive structures that are born out of fear and anger with compassion and love.

According to Father Keating, we should be open to receiving the compassion of divine mercy and become blameless and pure, enjoying the divine presence of whatever spiritual reality we identify with—because there are many different articulations of this reality. We need a practice that introduces us to silence.

Father Keating tells the story of a young man who enjoyed having fun, loved power and wealth, and liked to dominate others. He was proud of the fact he could drink his friends "under the table." But at some point in his life, he saw the error of his ways and decided to become a monk.

He joined a monastery and shared the monastic life with the other monks, praying and fasting every day. But then, he noticed that some monks started to disappear. Fewer monks were showing up for breakfast or for morning and evening prayer. At first, he didn't know why. But then, it hit him. He had fasted all the other monks "under the table." He wasn't developing his spirit or soul; he was competing to be the best monk.

According to Father Thomas Keating, "God's first language is silence." Whatever you call God or universal consciousness, one common step for all of these experiences is silence. We must still the chatter of our minds and go beyond our normal programmed thoughts, emotions, and beliefs to accomplish this. Stilling the mind can be achieved through meditation. Meditation is not just an Eastern practice. It is found in Christian communities where Christian mystics developed their own form of meditation.

Transcendent leadership is value-based and depends on the leader preaching and practicing values. Sharing these deeper values leads to higher motivation, commitment, and performance by the followers. Everyone envisions a better future and develops a higher level of self-worth.

As I mentioned in Chapter 1, in Maslow's books, *Motivation and Personality* and *Toward a Psychology of Being,* he discusses a 6th level in the hierarchy of needs, self-transcendence. At this level, developing spiritual awareness includes transformation, cohesion, inclusion, and unity.

The REAL leader has morality and a sense of ethics, a value system that is his or her internal compass. Learning to set and reset this compass to True North is what sets REAL leaders apart from would-be leaders. Developing the ability to share these values with others in an organization and to build a community of trust is what makes a servant leader great.

As a teacher and practitioner of Kundalini Yoga as taught by Yogi Bhajan, I've learned that you never stop learning in yoga. Yoga means to yoke or to join. It means finding that inner balance where your mind, body, emotions, and soul or spirit align. Many of us walk around disconnected from our inner world of thoughts, beliefs, and motives; and we react instead of create. In kundalini yoga practices, we develop our strengths as a yoga student and work to transcend our limitations and constrictions and become internally aligned.

When people think about yoga, they think about yoga poses. But to practice yoga means you practice releasing fears and limitations. You develop the practice of being grounded, centered, and still. You practice aligning your head and your heart until it becomes a habit and a state of being.

Physically, yoga builds inner strength and flexibility mentally, emotionally, and spiritually; yoga requires inner strength, agility, and discipline to maintain the practice. Ancient practices of yoga centered around spiritual connection and meditation. Yoga builds strength of character while learning how to bend and flex with life. That is why the word yoga means "to yoke or to join." Your outer personality and behavior become deeply connected with your internal True North, your inner wisdom.

Becoming quiet, still and centered internally is not easy. Our minds chatter all the time. Some forms of yogic breathing connect every exhalation to the letting go of all feelings of worry, concern, stress, and tension. With each inhale, with each inspiration, you sink deeper and deeper inside yourself. You do this until your inner world becomes peaceful and still and now, you exist only in the present moment. That's called yoga. That's called mindfulness.

Another practice to develop inner strength, agility, and flexibility is meditation. There are many definitions of meditation and mindfulness. Meditation is the ability to step back inside ourselves and become a witness to our inner stream of thoughts, motives, drivers, and the emotions behind our behavioral actions and reactions. Without awareness, we cannot change. Without awareness, we have no *choice*.

Mindfulness and meditation

An antidote to fear, and one of the most recent trends hitting businesses in terms of behavioral change, is *mindful meditation*. There are now hundreds of apps with meditative practices. One of my favorite apps is the Insight Timer. It has over 15,000 meditations ranging from stress reduction, to resilience, to sleep, to grief, to emotional stability, to reducing fear, to religious, to centeredness, to meditative music, to many others. The Insight Timer tracks how often you meditate. You can also set the duration of your meditation.

Another app that is quite popular is the 10% Happier app that teaches the basic skills of mindful meditation and moves you through various stages of meditation. Most business schools now have a consciousness or mindfulness aspect to their MBA programs.

As an executive coach and a facilitator of leadership programs, I teach mindfulness and meditation to nearly all my clients. I find it to be an indispensable tool to help with stress-mastery, reducing fear, and lowering reactive aggression levels.

Unfortunately, many of us are like the walking dead. So many people are so afraid of failing that they never try. Many of us fear rejection so much that we don't take risks lest people judge us. Meditation helps us develop resilience and overcome our fears.

During meditation, developing wisdom starts with letting go of old habits and programs and beginning each day anew with a beginner's mindset. One of the wisest things that a leader can say is, "I don't know, but I will find out." The conscious leader practices continual learning and insightfulness. They keep the door open to uncover the reality of any situation. Then, at the right moment, they will make wise choices. This is known as the moment of truth.

Conscious leaders develop wisdom using moments of truth to step back and practice mindfulness to clearly perceive and discern before making decisions.

The most successful leaders I've met in my life challenged themselves and others to break their own mold and become better human beings and better people. By pushing their boundaries, believing in themselves, and transcending their limitations, they grow and develop wisdom.

> *"The primary value in value-based leadership is other-centeredness - to be more concerned about other people and the organization than oneself. So, in other words, the leader's job is to fulfil the agenda, the role, and the vision of the organization, not his personal agenda. All the great leaders in the world are other-centered. The self-centered leader will derail in due course."*
>
> —**Dr John Ng**, *Unleashing the Greatness in You.*

In order to change, we must wake up and become conscious instead of acting, living, and behaving unconsciously. When leaders change, culture changes. Leaders carry a tremendous amount of power and influence, and rarely do they realize how much influence they have on others and the culture. If we are unaware and asleep, we can't change.

Mindfulness and stress reduction

Mindfulness as a meditative practice is the tool that helps leaders slow down inside and reflect before acting. This helps leaders act more purposefully and make better decisions. By quieting the mind and allowing ourselves to be more deeply aware of the present moment, we can start to become more mindful of our emotions, our thoughts, and how we react to stressful situations. Mindfulness, as a meditative practice, is a way of:

1. Relieving stress
2. Releasing emotional triggers that cause derailing behaviors
3. Gaining a broader perspective on the issues at hand
4. Finding new and transformative solutions

Stepping back and taking a non-judgmental, calm, and non-stressed perspective allows us to see ourselves and the situation in a new way. By observing the situation in a non-judgmental way and without our biases allows us to find innovative solutions.

These practices are no longer outside the mainstream. Mindfulness and meditation have become mainstream. As Monica Thakrar of the Forbes Council points out, "Large companies, such as Google, Aetna, and General Mills, have been implementing large-scale mindfulness programs over the past few years." She notes that thousands of employees have gone through these corporate-sponsored programs, and data indicates that practicing mindfulness accounts for definite improvements, including increased productivity, faster, more effective decision-making, improved listening skills, and reduced stress levels (Thakrar, Monica. June 2017. *Forbes.*).

Aetna, a pioneer in mindfulness-based training, found that "team members who participated in the training (mindfulness training) added roughly 60 minutes of productivity per week, which they calculated was worth about $3,000 per year per team member" (Aetna. December 2017. 4 ways mindfulness improves your productivity. *Huffington Post.*).

As an executive consultant, a yoga practitioner, and a meditation teacher, I find that when I help managers and leaders develop a mindful, heart-based, meditative practice, they become more:

1. Compassionate
2. Empathetic
3. Confident
4. Peaceful
5. Secure

Developing these qualities helps leaders gain a deeper perspective on the issues they face. They can better balance leading with heart while driving for results. In the next chapter, we discuss how REAL leadership creates high-performing organizational culture.

CHAPTER 8

REAL CULTURE

"We can change culture if we change behavior."
—**Dr. Aubrey Daniels,** *Founder ADI.*

What is culture? Why is it important? Does organizational culture make a difference in performance? What is a good culture? What is a bad culture?

Culture is best defined as the behavioral interaction between people. It is the social fabric and the behavioral glue that binds an organization together. Culture is the internal eco-system of organizational purpose, values, behaviors, and goals. Culture is the human operating system of any organization. It is the human side of business. Depending on how well organizations manage the human factor, this determines if culture creates a competitive advantage or not.

The REAL leadership model, as outlined in the previous chapters, emphasizes the importance of engagement and agility for improved organizational results. Companies lose or gain their competitive advantage, in part, by how well-aligned people are and how agile, flexible and innovative the organization is.

If culture is the human side of business, then how do you leverage culture to create the competitive advantage? Creating the cultural competitive advantage starts with understanding that leadership behaviors shape the actual culture of an organization. Having worked in many organizations over the past 30 years, I can share with you that REAL leaders drive REAL culture and gain REAL results.

Strong organizational cultures start with a well-defined vision and clearly articulated values. The purpose, vision, and values of a company are unique for each company. This uniqueness is what many senior leaders believe will give their company the competitive advantage. Organizations with high-performing cultures have strong brands and reputations with employees and customers. Leadership defines behavioral and leadership competencies that embody the vision and values needed to align culture with strategy.

Many organizations annually assess the effectiveness of their culture. Working with executive teams, I've found that there are four major hindrances to cultural effectiveness. They are:

1. Lack of communication and feedback
2. Lack of engagement
3. Lack of alignment
4. Lack of agility

Organizations with REAL conscious cultures instill a sense of fearlessness, openness, and transparency to overcome these hindrances. The open-door policy is truly an open door. Differing perspectives are not only valued but encouraged. Conscious cultures focus on delivering meaning and purpose for their employees and community at large. By focusing on meaning and purpose, the brand takes care of itself.

Years ago, I worked with the leadership team of an operating center in Texas. Their leader, Laura, exemplified REAL leadership characteristics, and in her center, they created a REAL culture. When I first met the team, two of the most senior directors were at each other's throats. The continual bickering and competition between the two created a hostile work environment. We worked together to get to the source of the issues. If we didn't resolve the conflict, one or both would have been fired. Their battle went back several years, and each had their list of grievances against the other. While it wasn't easy, we respectfully laid out all the issues: the good, the bad, and the ugly.

The two leaders had to drop their ego-centric behaviors, grow up, and forgive. As we worked through each issue one-by-one, their defenses dropped. Blame was eliminated. The team went through a transcendent experience with each other as they let go of all the old behaviors and decided they would operate in a new, more healthy and respectful way. We came up with the team behavioral agreement, the action plans for improved teamwork and cultural effectiveness, and each member on the team had their individual action plan.

Although I coached Laura, I did not see the team again until six months later. When the team got together, I noticed they had a new mantra: "I've got you." When a contentious issue would come to the table, they would remind each other that they had each other's back. "I got you." Over the next three years, this team out-performed all the other worldwide operation centers in their company, and three people from the group were promoted.

This company had its values, mission, and purpose, but it was Laura and her team who created the cultural glue that made the difference.

Harvard Business Review published an article, "*How Company Culture Shapes Employee Motivation.*" Researchers and authors Lindsey McGregor and Neel Doshi found after "surveying over 20,000 workers, analyzing 50 major companies, and conducting scores of experiments and scouring the landscape of academic resources, they came to one conclusion, "why we work determines how well we work." (2015)

According to research by Kotter & Heskett (*Corporate Culture and Performance*), companies whose culture emphasizes the leadership impact on customers, stockholders, and employees improved significantly on their long-term performance and produced a much larger margin than companies without this culture.

- Revenue was 4.1 times higher (682% vs. 166%);
- Stock price was 12.2 time higher (901% vs. 74%);
- Net income was 756% improvement vs. 1%; ROI was 15 times higher.

As you can see from the above study, how leaders behave strongly influences culture and organizational results. REAL leaders understand that their behavior impacts culture and they work actively to improve their leadership people skills.

Changing Culture

During the last 30 years working in the field of organizational development and executive coaching, I've seen that more and more leaders are concerned about culture and how to improve it. Many of my conversations start with, "How do I?" While there are many topics and many themes, the primary theme of the "how do I" questions center around themes of culture, leadership, behavior, conflict, breaking down silos, and improving performance. Here is a list of typical questions:

1. How do I change my culture?
2. How do I improve leadership effectiveness?
3. How do I improve engagement and performance?
4. How do I handle this cultural or behavioral issue?
5. How do I deal with this person?
6. How do I drive buy-in?
7. How do I become the best leader I can be?

These questions are difficult to answer, though there is a foundation that I use as a springboard when I answer them: *It starts with emotional intelligence based on Consciousness and Awareness.* Laura and her team created a high-performance culture by first having everyone work on their self-awareness and self-management skills. They proactively changed how they engaged with each other and with all the team members in the operating center. They encouraged agility and allowed mistakes. Through that, they grew, matured, and developed a new level of wisdom. They improved their employee satisfaction scores and had the best customer satisfaction scores.

Conscious cultures start with conscious leaders

We know that organizational culture has a significant impact on employee engagement and business performance. In a six-part series on the CEO's Role in Shaping Organizational Culture, *Chief Executive Magazine* found that the most important thing a leader does "is shape and reinforce the organization's culture." This, therefore, should not be underestimated when evaluating your role as a leader.

Have you ever experienced working on a team where everyone had each other's backs? Where constructive feedback was used as an opportunity for growth rather than something to be afraid of? Where successes were celebrated? Where open dialog and discussion were expected? And where people collaborated to find the best solution rather than compete against each other for territory or power?

If you answered "yes" to these questions, then you have the ingredients of a conscious culture. It generally means that the manager or the leader encouraged this type of atmosphere. This is the type of culture Laura and her team created.

If an organization has a culture of silo behavior and internal competition, decision-making is often affected adversely. This impacts the workforce in carrying out tasks effectively, which is detrimental to the business. If an organization suffers from a *shoot-the-messenger* climate, leadership misses the opportunity to change and correct the direction of the company. If you have experienced this type of culture, it most likely is due, at least in part, to a leader creating this type of culture. Therefore, it is important to build a conscious culture.

Culture, leadership, and performance

To improve organizational results, start with leadership. As you can see from the illustration, leaders drive engagement and culture, instill purpose, set strategy, and provide the glue to align people, processes, and innovation. Based on recent research, we know that organizational culture is linked to organizational performance. As you can see from the illustration, you can focus on improving *process*, but that is only 1/3 of the performance equation. You can change and improve *strategy and purpose,* but that accounts for only 1/3 of the performance equation. People must actually *perform* together to improve performance. No matter what values, mission, purpose, strategy, process, or methodologies are espoused, people must *buy-in* into these ideas and agree to perform. This is how leadership shapes culture for improved performance.

Based on a study by McKinsey, we know that "70 percent of change programs fail to achieve their goals, largely due to employee resistance and lack of management support. We also know that when people are truly invested in change, it is 30 percent more likely to stick." So, why don't management-change programs and culture-change programs stick? Because we must look at the *people side* of how work gets done as well as the processes, methodology, strategy, and vision.

It is unfortunate that many senior leaders are protected and insulated from negative news. They are given what they want to hear rather than what they need to hear. REAL leaders know that this tendency exists and make every effort to understand the "truth" of the organization, no matter how difficult. Rather than shoot the messenger, they welcome the bad news and view it as an opportunity to grow and develop the culture. This is the essence of culture, our behavior, and how we communicate and relate to each other.

How work gets done depends on teamwork, communication, trust, transparency, collaboration, and idea generation. It depends on how well people work together and how well leadership models these behaviors. Leadership also needs to hold themselves and their people accountable for living and breathing these values and ways of being.

Take Pixar Studios, for example. Their corporate

philosophy puts value on cooperative organizational culture. Ed Catmull was a computer graphics scientist working at the New York Institute of Technology (NYIT) when he was hired in 1979 by Lucasfilm Ltd. to lead its computer division. Five years later, John Lasseter, who had been an animator at Disney, joined him at Lucasfilm. The two were with the company in 1986 when it spun off an independent business with controlling interest, owned by Apple co-founder Steve Jobs. The new company was called Pixar, with Catmull designated as President.

In 2006, Pixar was sold to the Walt Disney Company, and Catmull became president of both Walt Disney Animation Studios and Pixar Animation Studios, and Lasseter became the chief creative officer of both studios. It was in this environment that the two would create an organizational culture of trust, respect, and mutual support that would set them apart from all other studios.

As Catmull said, "Of great importance—and something that sets us apart from other studios—is the way people at all levels support one another. Everyone is fully invested in helping everyone else turn out the best work. They really do feel that it's all for one and one for all." Catmull recognized that managers cannot mandate cooperation among workers. Working together takes trust and respect, and these must be aimed toward and earned over time. (*Harvard Business Review*, 2008).

According to Gallup, "70% of variance in employee performance has to do with the relationship with their managers" (Gallup's *State of the American manager: Analytic and advice for leader*). This variation is, in turn, responsible for severely low worldwide employee engagement. A Gallup study reported that "only 30% of U.S. employees are engaged at work, and a staggering low 13% worldwide are engaged." Even worse, over the past 12 years, these low numbers have barely budged, meaning that most employees worldwide are failing to develop and contribute at work.

At Pixar, employees are encouraged to approach anyone in any department to help solve problems. They don't have to go through "proper" channels because Pixar recognizes there is a difference between the decision-making hierarchy and the communications structure of the organization. Communication needs to be open and free.

This means that managers do not have tight controls over their employees and do not micromanage them. Managers do not have to give permission for their employees to brainstorm or gather together to generate new ideas. Managers do not have to be the first to know about new ideas. As Pixar's Catmull puts it, "It's okay for managers to walk into a meeting and be surprised."

The design of the Pixar building is itself a testament to open communications, conceived by Steve Jobs. It is structured for maximum social interaction and "inadvertent encounters." The center of the building is a large atrium containing the cafeteria, meeting rooms, mailboxes, and bathrooms. As a result, everyone goes there several times a day, and there is a strong possibility of interaction. Chance encounters are highly valued. Leaders encourage and support the engagement of everyone in the organization with the result being more creativity and overall effectiveness.

As in the Pixar example, communication and engagement are highly valued, along with taking risk and recovering from failure. A prerequisite for strong communication, deep engagement, risk-taking, and recovering from failure is transparency and honesty.

Direct honesty is another antidote for fear. When we are directly honest and transparent, we stop deluding ourselves and confront the issues head-on. Direct honesty and transparency can be difficult, especially if we need to provide difficult feedback or if we disagree; however, if we aren't transparent and honest, issues fester. If we allow fear to keep us quiet and put heads in the sand, we cannot innovate, create, or change. Therefore, it is imperative to be directly honest about your people skills, emotional intelligence, and your leadership effectiveness.

Becoming conscious and aware leads to inner freedom. When we become conscious of our leadership behaviors, our positive strengths, and how we derail, we have the moment of truth where we are free to choose to change or remain the same. If we remain unaware, we are not free to make choices and are doomed to live out of our programmed habits and behaviors. If we remain the same, we will continue to obtain the same results. If we change, we can create change in our personal lives and as leaders, which can impact organizational performance positively.

The ABC's of Conscious Culture change

Conscious culture change requires work on both the systemic side of the organization and the human side of the organization. Here are five steps of Conscious culture change. Each step is composed of three sub-steps. Two-thirds of the sub-steps involve methodologies, processes, efficiencies, and definition. One-third of conscious cultural transformation has to do with creating the glue that holds it all together. For the purposes of this book, I will focus on the human side, the social glue of culture.

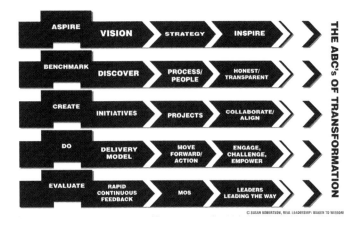

C SUSAN ROBERTSON, REAL LEADERSHIP: WAKEN TO WISDOM

Aspire

Employees need to be inspired if they are going to aspire. Creating an aspirational vision of the future requires a deep exploration of the business values. An aspirational vision must define exactly what the company stands for. Some companies are known for their controlling environment, whereas others are known for their creative culture. A good example of an aspirational vision and culture is Tentree, a company known for its high-quality organic clothing and environmental awareness. For every item purchased, 10 trees are planted. This helps to create a sustainable vision for the future, making employees proud to work for them, leading to a productive work environment.

But let's say you are the leader of a department rather than a C-Suite executive; how do you create an aspirational vision that inspires? I worked with a leader who decided it was her role and duty to figure out how to shave an average of five hours a week off her manager's regular worktime. Typically, the managers of her department worked 55-60 hours per week. When the team talked about how to shave five hours a week off for everyone, there was a transformation. Collaboratively, they were inspired and accomplished their goal. They became more efficient and creative and became better leaders. Within 18 months, 90% of the team got promoted.

Benchmark

Once you set the direction and people are inspired to create and work toward your desired future, it's crucial to benchmark your organization. The discovery process must include identifying the strengths and gaps in both the processes and in your people. This way, you know your starting point to implement the vision you are creating. It is imperative to participate in honest and transparent discussion with bosses and peers and prepare honest reports about the internal nature of the organization.

Create

You know the direction, you know your starting point in the culture, and you know the capabilities of your leaders. Now, you must create the initiatives and projects using collaboration and alignment to ensure you get the results you desire. Creating and aligning at the people level involves discovering a variety of solutions. Bring the team together and dialog on how to collaborate and align. By now, you know I like to use sports analogies. In basketball, each person has the role and position they play. The magic comes in how well they execute their team strategy. Collaboration and alignment are determined on how well they pass the ball between each other. The magic happens because the team creates and practices how they will align and pass the ball. In business, this is known as your team agreement. In the earlier example of Laura and her team, they decided to create a supportive culture where everyone had the opportunity to grow and develop. They decided to create a culture where differing views were welcomed and challenged in a healthy way. As a leader, involve your team in the creation process of how to work together.

Do

As leaders, it's important to engage, challenge, and empower employees. This allows them to utilize and refine their creative problem-solving abilities, which will keep them engaged. If leadership micromanages every step, then the organization is only as good as one brain. People want to be challenged; they want responsibility, and they want to know they can make a difference. Giving away power through engagement is a key leadership skill and allows a collective of influences to exert control over an organization, which will benefit it in the long run.

Evaluate

Very few things go right the first time. It's therefore important to review the organizational transformation from the perspectives of the overall culture and leadership. What's working? What isn't? What needs to be changed? Leaders must consciously lead this type of environment. Evaluation doesn't mean just figuring out what went wrong; it also means figuring out what went right and learning from it all.

Conscious Culture and the bottom line

To build a conscious culture, we start with becoming conscious and aware leaders, driving consciousness throughout the organization. This means creating programs that instill mindfulness at all levels of the organization. Helping teams achieve Shuniya opens the doors to innovation and creativity.

In business today, we see the movement toward mindfulness and contemplation. Leaders of organizations are recognizing that practicing mindfulness and meditation helps organizations win. Typically, businesses are finding that when they make mindfulness and meditation a priority and create meditative spaces in their organization, productivity, and presenteeism goes up. Decision-making becomes more efficient. Collaboration improves.

Andy Lee, Aetna's Chief Mindfulness Officer, talks about Aetna mindfulness initiatives: mindfulness month, mindfulness associates, and the mindfulness center in Hartford. He discusses embedding mindfulness into a corporate culture. As a result of their cultural mindfulness practices, Aetna has been able to measure real bottom-line impacts.

He cites the benefits of mindfulness programs as:

- $3,000 per year increase in productivity per person per year

- 28% reduction in perceived stress level
- 20% improvement in overall sleep quality
- 19% reduction in pain level

Why does this happen? When leaders and employees learn the art of "no-thing-ness" through mindfulness practices, they become mindful, humble servants, and they lead from a sense of selflessness and ego-lessness. They build cultures where employees flourish and agility and engagement increase. When this happens, profitability improves.

David Gelles shares these conclusions about insurance giant Aetna in his book, *Mindful Work:*

- A highly stressed employee costs the company an extra $2,000 per year in healthcare, when compared to their less-stressed peers.
- Health care costs at Aetna—which total more than $90 million a year—are going down now that they offer mindfulness programs.
- In 2012, as mindfulness programs ramped up, health care costs fell a total of 7%. (That equals $6.3 million going straight to the bottom line, partly attributed to mindfulness training.)
- Aetna calculated that productivity gains alone were about $3,000 per employee, equaling an 11:1 return on investment.

Gelles stated, "This study is just one example of how the benefits of mindfulness training programs, which utilize mindfulness meditation, can be quantifiable. Consistently, mindfulness has been shown to serve as a method of relieving employee stress and encouraging increased productivity."

Conscious, transcendent cultures are achieved when people work in unison and have each other's backs. The workforce in a transcendent culture knows they are creating and striving toward something bigger and something more meaningful. When we learn to become more agile—because every day is an unknown—and we are open to deeper guidance as leaders, we stop acting from our ego-based fears and start leading from transcendent consciousness. This drives cultural change.

Transforming corporate cultures

The study of transcendence and consciousness has been around for thousands of years, in many forms. The fact that businesses are now understanding the importance of conscious awakening shows the growth of human evolution. What was once esoteric and confined to the realm of religion now transcends into mainstream business practices.

In the book, *Conscious Business*, Fred Kofman describes conscious culture transformation like this: "To change a culture, the leaders have to change the messages people receive about what they must do to fit in. When people understand that there are new requirements for belonging, they adjust their behavior accordingly. Cultural change starts with a new set of messages. Culture-changing communication is nonverbal—the "doing" rather than the "saying"—and comes most vividly from leadership behaviors. The behavior of leaders exemplifies what people with power—and those who aspire to have it—are supposed to do. A small change in a senior manager's behavior can send a big message."

Messages that leaders send are not just spoken words or words hanging on a banner, messages from leaders come in the form of what people say and—more importantly—what people do. Leadership behavior is the message. Looking back at the evolution of awareness, consciousness, and connected spirituality, what they have in common is a sense of self-transcendence. When we transcend our programmed selves, we are in a better position to lead others through transcendence and change. Transcendence changes culture.

Eileen Fisher is a clothing designer and owner of a $450 million clothing franchise. She is a firm adherent to meditation and mindfulness. It is a significant part of her company culture. To say that "the 66-year-old clothing designer is an advocate of mindfulness practices would be something of an understatement. Fisher believes businesses that take the time to be more thoughtful about what they're doing can effect real positive change within the business, industry, and throughout the world" (*Business Insider*).

Fisher instituted a moment of silence and, "Since instituting the moment of silence," Fisher said she's seen a deepening of the work, a greater sense of purpose among her employees, and people making more conscious choices about what they're doing and how they can change the "nasty fashion industry. Across the company—designers and merchandisers and advertising people and people in the supply chain—the passion around this work has gotten a lot deeper." This is the business version of Shuniya, which enables her workforce to reach the still point and by doing so, Fisher activates deeper passion and creativity in her entire workforce.

Another example of mindfulness, meditation, and Shuniya at work is the practices of happiness at Google. All Google employees are given the opportunity to learn meditation and mindfulness. One of the job perks at Google is that its 52,000 employees are given free lessons in mindfulness. Google's meditation guru, known formally as the "Jolly Good Fellow," Chade-Meng Tan, has hefty responsibilities, as his official job description is to "enlighten minds, open hearts, (and) create world peace." Some meetings at Google start out with a couple of minutes of meditation. Not only does adding meditation to the workday make people happier and more present, but it also makes people more productive. The trick, says Tan, is to "get into that frame of mind on demand," and meditation teaches people to do exactly this.

Even the Wharton School of Business has gotten into mindfulness and meditation. In an article from the Wharton School of Business website, there is a description of the importance of these ancient techniques for dealing with the modern age:

"Mindfulness is a centuries-old idea that has been reinvented to address the challenges of our digital age. Mindfulness describes a state of being present in the moment and leaving behind one's tendency to judge. It allows one to pause amid the constant inflow of stimuli and consciously decide how to act, rather than react reflexively with ingrained behavior patterns. Mindfulness, therefore, is perfectly suited to counterbalance the digital-age challenges of information overload and constant distraction."

"The benefits of mindfulness are both clear and proven. Mindfulness programs help leaders and employees reflect effectively, focus sharply on the task at hand, master peak levels of stress, and recharge quickly. On an organizational level, mindfulness reduces sick days, increases trust in leadership, and boosts employee engagement. What's more, mindfulness helps to unlock the full potential of digital and agile transformations. New processes and structures are just the starting points for these transformations." (How companies can instill mindfulness. *Knowledge Wharton.*).

As leaders recognize the need to develop conscious business practices, they also embrace taking better care of their people. As seen in the Aetna example, a highly stressed employee can cost the company as much as $2000 per year. Adopting the practices of mindfulness, yoga, and stress reduction, Aetna has seen their productivity go up and are achieving an 11:1 return on investment for their training programs. When an organization adopts consciousness and conscious well-being for everyone, the evidence is clear: the bottom-line improves.

Chapter 9

Conclusion

Transcending your personal limitations and beliefs and tapping into your deeper intuition and insight is the journey of becoming an aware, conscious, and REAL leader. What leaders do, the decisions they make, and the skills they apply at work is important. How leaders act and behave is fundamentally important to creating conscious cultures, driving deep engagement, and positively affecting the bottom-line of the company. The skills required to be an effective leader are business and strategic intelligence and REAL leadership.

The difference between having business and strategic intelligence and being a REAL leader is: that business and strategic intelligence is based on education, acquired knowledge and learning through experience. All of this is based on our wiring of what we were taught, experienced, and learned. As a result, our internal CPU is coded with a lot of biases, stereotypes, fears, and habitual thinking patterns.

REAL leadership and deep wisdom are about moving beyond the known so that you can creatively use your business and strategic intelligence with the wisdom and discernment to know what decisions to make. REAL leadership is wisdom and the fearlessness to take risks to be innovative and creative, while deeply inspiring others to make a difference. When leaders bring these two sets of skills together–strategic intelligence and REAL leadership–they generate a powerful culture, increase employee engagement, increase measurable bottom-line results, and make a difference in the world.

Only recently has leadership wisdom and awakened leadership been studied as a key quality for effective leadership. From my personal experience as a coach and a cultural change expert, leaders who display the qualities associated with leadership wisdom (compassion, authenticity, transparency, humility, integrity, and discernment) drive higher results. They drive higher results because they are willing to face their limitations honestly, and then, they take themselves through the process of inner examination and inner transformation. This helps REAL leaders create enhanced emotional intelligence, improved self-management leading to mastering fear, and leading with humility and authenticity. As REAL leaders value their own inner transformation and growth, they promote the personal transformation and development of others. REAL leaders lead with transcendent consciousness.

This book is a backpack of R.E.A.L. tools to help you develop wisdom, and become a conscious, transcendent and REAL leader. The world needs wise leaders, wise decisions, with concern for others and for the future of humanity. We have our individual beliefs and dreams. We have common experiences and feelings. The desire to share with others is what makes us human. As a leader in your own organization, you can realize true achievement by simply acknowledging and supporting the humanness you see. Treating people as people first and as workers second is building an organization on shared values. That is as strong a foundation as you can have.

Your organization can be a high-performing, vibrant team of contributors, individually and collectively engaged in a mutual quest for reaching and surpassing all goals placed before them. You and they can enjoy a culture of organizational success on a scale never before achieved in your company. This success will be realized through a transcendence from old habits and unconscious behaviors to a new openness and state of being *at choice* to do better.

Transcendence requires leadership wisdom. REAL leaders, who care about humanity, are self-less and work for the greater good. REAL leaders are fully conscious of the need to let go of egos while caring for others and inspiring them to share their ideas and skills to be all that they can be. REAL leaders need R.E.A.L. tools for developing this consciousness, this awareness, and this leadership wisdom to take them along the journey of discovery and guide others on their road of discovery and transformation.

REAL, conscious, and aware leaders consistently cultivate wisdom.

Using these tools, you will change your own life, as well as mold your teams into powerful, willing forces for accomplishment and growth. You will unleash their creativity, excite their passions, free their imaginations, raise their energy levels, encourage sharing, instill confidence, and enable them to reach their full potential.

My recommendation is to use the tools in the backpack. Learn to be a conscious leader and learn to identify consciousness—and the lack thereof—in your organization. Wherever you see trouble lurking, try to discern whether the individuals are being honest, transparent, caring for each other, and trusting or showing that they have self-interest and private agendas. Discern whether they are acting out of fear, habits, or bias.

Only REAL leaders can know if they are being honest with themselves. And only REAL leaders can sense whether others are being honest with themselves. There are visible signs of dysfunction in many organizations, and there are also subtler signs that may not be so visible. Individuals, teams, and entire organizations can be asleep, unconscious, unaware, uninspired, unhappy, and unproductive.

Only REAL leaders can wake themselves and their company to wisdom.

Notes

Sources for the journey

Kofman, F., *Conscious Business: How to Build Value through Values*

Dispenza, J., *Breaking the Habit of Being the Yourself: How to Lose Your Mind and Create a New One.*

Sources for chapter 1

Maslow, A *Theory of Human Motivation*

Maslow, A., *What is self-transcendence? Positive Psychology*

Crossan, M., Vera, D., Nanjad, L., *Transcendent Leadership: Strategic Leadership in Dynamic Environments. CT Bauer College of Business, The University of Houston, TX. USA. The Leadership Quarterly 19, 2008.*

https://www.forbes.com/sites/forbescoachescouncil/2017/05/11/six-keys-to-transcendent-leadership/#669904c07e2d

https://positivepsychologyprogram.com/self-transcendence/

http://www.drpaulwong.com/meaning-seeking-self-transcendence-and-well-being/

Sources for chapter 2

Catmull, E., *Harvard Business Review*, 2008

Keller, S., Price, C., *Beyond Performance: How Great Organizations Build Ultimate Competitive Advantage.* Wiley. Times Group Books. New Delhi. 2016.

Moline, P., *We're far more afraid of failure than ghosts:*

Here's how to stare it down. Health & Wellness, Los
Angeles Times, Oct., 2015

Dotlich, D. L., and Cairo, P. C., *Why CEO's Fail.* Jossey-
Bass: A Wiley Imprint. Copyright 2003. San Francisco

https://www.hrmagazine.co.uk/article-details/bad-
company-culture-costs-uk-economy-23-3-billion

https://www.mckinsey.com/featured-
insights/leadership/changing-change-management

https://news.gallup.com/businessjournal/182792/managers
-account-variance-employee-engagement.aspx

Sources for chapter 3

Ledesma, J. *Conceptual Frameworks and Research Models on
Resilience in Leadership.* 2014. SAGE Open Patterson, J.
L., & Kelleher, P. *Resilient school leaders: Strategies for
turning adversity into achievement.* 2005. Association for
Supervision and Curriculum Development, Alexandria,
VA

Howard, C. S., & Irving, J. A. The Impact of Obstacles
and Developmental Experiences on Resilience in
Leadership Formation. *Proceedings of the American
Society for Business and Behavioral Sciences.* 2013.

Sources for chapter 4

Enes, K. and Şengüllendi, Fatih, *Transformational
Leadership and Organizational Innovation: The
Mediating Role of Positive Psychological Capital,* 2018.

Bass, Bernard M., Center for Leadership Studies,
Binghamton University, and Riggio, Ronald E., Kravis
Leadership Institute, Claremont McKenna College,

Transformational Leadership, Second Edition 2006.
Lawrence Erlbaum Associates. Mahwah, New Jersey.

Sull, D., Homkes, R., and Sull, C. March 2015. Why strategy execution unravels and what to do about it. *Harvard Business Review*

https://hbr.org/2018/07/do-your-employees-feel-respected

https://www.i4cp.com/member/restricted?referer=%2Fsurvey-analyses%2Fpurposeful- collaboration-the-essential-components-of-collaborative-cultures

Sources for chapter 5

Zenger, J. and Folkman, J., *How Managers Drive Results and Employee Engagement at the Same Time*, Harvard Business Review, June 19, 2017

Pfeffer, J., *What Were They Thinking? Unconventional Wisdom About Management*, Joiner and Josephs, *Leadership Agility*, 2007

Goleman, D. August 2017. *Leaders who get their teams.* Korn Ferry Institute.

Sources for chapter 6

Jinhyung, K. et al, *Approaching the True Self: Promotion Focus Predicts the Experience of Authenticity,* Journal of Research in Personality, Elsevier, (Accessed from researchgate.net, Dec. 28, 2018).

Brown, M. E., and Trevino, L. K., *Ethical Leadership: A review and future directions,* the Sam and Irene Black School of Business, Pennsylvania State University, Erie, PA. The Leadership Quarterly. Elsevier. 2006. Retrieved from ScienceDirect.com Dec. 29, 2018.

The Authentic Personality: A Theoretical and Empirical Conceptualization and the Development of the Authenticity Scale, Journal of Counseling Psychology. 2008.

Seppaia, E. M., *Compassion: Our First Instinct*, Psychology Today, June 2013.

Cashman, K., *Success: 8 Principles of Purpose-Driven Leadership*, 2017.

Walumbwa, F., Avolio, B., Gardner, W., Wernsing, T., Peterson. S., *Authentic Leadership: Validation of Theory Based Measure*, University of Nebraska-Lincoln, Management Department of Faculty Publications, February 2008. https://digitalcommons.unl.edu/cgi/viewcontent.cgi?article=1021&context=managementfacpu b

Thompson, M., *What Does Wise Leadership Mean*. April 15, 2013. https://www.iedp.com/articles/what-does-wise-leadership-mean/

Pires, Fernanda B.C., *Self-compassion is associated with less stress and depression and greater attention and brain response to affective stimuli in women managers,* BMC Women's Health. 2018

Sources for chapter 7

Covey, S. R., *The 7 habits of highly effective people*, Free Press; New York, NY, 1989

Covey, S. R., *Principle-centered leadership*, Fireside Books, Simon and Schuster; New York, NY, 1990

Maslow, A. H., *Motivation and personality*, Harper; New York, NY, 1954.

Maslow, A. H., *Toward a psychology of being*, D. Van
    Nostrand Company; New York, NY, 1968

Sanders, J. O., *Spiritual Leadership: Principles of Excellence
    for Every Believer*, 1967, 1980, 1994, 2007, The Moody
    Bible Institute of Chicago.

Hanson, R. and Mendius, R., *Buddha's Brain. The
    Practical Neuroscience of Happiness, Love and Wisdom.*

http://upliftconnect.com/neuroscience-of-singing/

https://qz.com/506229/neuroscience-backs-up-the-
    buddhist-belief-that-the-self-isnt-constant-but-ever-
    changing/

https://www.psychologytoday.com/us/blog/out-the-
    darkness/201704/the-self-is-not- illusion

https://www.3ho.org/community/your-stories/shuniya-
    point-stillness-lifestyle

https://www.ncbi.nlm.nih.gov/pmc/articles/PMC5038601

Sources for chapter 8

Kofman, F., *Conscious Business*

Gillet, R., *Eileen-fisher-starts-every-meeting-with-meditation*,
    Business Insider, Nov. 4, 2016.

Kotter, J. P. and Heskett, J. L. 1992. *Corporate Culture and
    Performance.* Free Press; New York, NY

Shen, G. and Chen, B. 2010. Developing a unique
    corporate culture: How a small company can use that
    for sustainable growth. *Minority and Small Business
    Review*

https://www.diamondway-
    buddhism.org/buddhism/buddha/

https://www.britannica.com/topic/monasticism/Varieties-

of-monasticism-in-the-religions-of-the-
world#ref422819

https://www.ancient.eu/Taoism/

https://dailystoic.com/what-is-stoicism-a-definition-3-
stoic-exercises-to-get-you-started/

https://www.businessinsider.com/eileen-fisher-starts-every-
meeting-with-meditation-2016-11

https://www.forbes.com/sites/alicegwalton/2014/12/14/60
-minutes-explores-the-rise-of- mindfulness-meditation-
and-how-it-can-change-the-brain/

http://knowledge.wharton.upenn.edu/article/how-
companies-can-instill-mindfulness/

About the Author

Susan Robertson is co-founder and managing partner at Stop At Nothing, an organizational transformation and leadership consulting firm she began with her husband, Barry Robertson, over 30 years ago. Working with over 35,000 leaders in over 30 countries, the company helps leaders transform their corporate cultures by enhancing leadership effectiveness. Stop At Nothing provides executive leadership coaching and mentoring, strategic consulting, five-day leadership programs, and cultural transformation for organizations seeking to improve engagement and culture and drive peak performance.

More recently, Susan Robertson, along with her husband and two other business partners—Kevin and Andrea Haas—founded *Conscious Business Insights*, an organization dedicated to creating REAL leaders and Conscious Cultures using digital technology. In her early 20s, she had two transformative experiences that changed her life. She attended a transformational, self-awareness-based leadership workshop and, that same year, she had a near-death white-water-rafting experience—and with that, she changed her life. She left her safe banking career and co-founded Stop At Nothing. She continues to explore clinical and transpersonal psychology, behavioral sciences, neurofeedback, re-decision therapy, and other psychological modalities to build the educational foundation and experience that allows her help leaders build highly effective organizations and highly effective leaders.

As part of her mission and purpose in life, she wants to help others find that transformative moment in their lives that allow them to find their true passion and purpose in life. That is what inspired her and Barry to co-found Stop At Nothing.

Susan loves facilitating the leadership programs for large and small businesses. She has worked with several family businesses, helping them deal with family dynamics while running the business. She has also coached executive women to reach higher levels in major organizations. Susan enjoys the challenge of helping teams transform and become high-performing. She believes that helping leaders change, changes the world.

Ever a student and a teacher, Susan continually challenges herself to learn and grow. Susan is a certified Registered Yoga Teacher of Kundalini Yoga, Restorative, and Chair Yoga. Her current passion is researching and exploring neuroscience and how neuroplasticity in the brain can help create behavioral change. Additionally, she loves researching studies on how mindfulness, meditation, and yoga impact the neurobiology and neurological wiring and their impact to stress-related behaviors (derailers). Susan uses this research to help her clients make the changes they want to make. In her spare time, she enjoys reading, meditating, snow-skiing, hiking, and teaching yoga meditation. Her most important love is spending time with her husband, four step-children, and seven grandchildren.

ABOUT THE BOOK

REAL Leadership: Waking to Wisdom

Leaders today are often unconscious and unaware of how their learned fears, egos, and personality flaws adversely affect their effectiveness in dealing with others. Their followers are not engaged, not motivated, and not performing at their best. Leaders need to be authentic, manage from their hearts, be consistent with their beliefs, emanate trust and transparency, and allow their followers to be free to create, share, and excel at what they do best.

In *REAL Leadership: Waking to Wisdom*, Susan Robertson takes readers on a journey from being unconscious and blithely going through the motions of leadership—driven by harmful habits—to an awakening of inner truth, resiliency, engagement, authenticity, and leadership wisdom–REAL leadership.

Referencing research and 30 years' worth of experience in leadership consulting and organizational and cultural transformation, Robertson shows why leaders fail, why fear prevents leaders from really fulfilling their potential, and how they can recover through techniques of self-awareness and self-management. She also illustrates the impact leadership has on high- versus low-performing cultures.

While there are many books out there on how to manage better, there are few, if any, that talk about changing from within. Robertson addresses the transformative process that helps leaders change their self-image, reframe their minds, awake spiritually, find inner truth and honesty, and achieve a level of transcendence–all critical elements of leadership wisdom.

For individual leaders, teams, and organizations, *REAL Leadership: Waking to Wisdom* is a valuable tool for learning how to change the very nature of our inner being, become conscious, healthy, and well-adjusted, and bring a positive energy to everything we do in life.

Based on principles such as mutual respect and caring, Robertson's philosophy is a welcome change in management doctrine. It's management for better organizational accomplishment as well as for the greater good of the individual and, by extension, society in general.

Acknowledgements

There have been so many teachers and mentors in my life that because of their support, knowledge, and inspiration in my life, I've been challenged and have had the ability to grow and heal. To my step-children, Bert, Drew, Didi, and Laura and my daughter-in-law Megan: thank you for allowing me to be part of your lives and for all the love. You have been amazing teachers to me. Thank you to my mother, Phyllis O'Hara. Although there were difficulties, there were joys, too. Thank you to my father, Cesar Calma, for listening to me and helping me heal. Thank you to my teacher, Edward Bujdos, who started me on my healing journey, who first introduced me to meditation, breathwork, and to emotional healing. Thank you to Sister Marie, who always inspired us, her students, to reach beyond our limitations and reach for the stars. Thank you to my dear friends, Tsolagiu and Rahkwees Keh, for your guidance in teaching me how to be a REAL human being and helping me move beyond my ego-based fears to become more compassionate, authentic, transparent, and real.

I must thank my business partners at Stop At Nothing, Ted and Nancy Powell, Kevin and Andrea Haas, Jon and Tina Patton, and all of the people who worked at Stop At Nothing or who have been associated with Stop At Nothing. Without the team and all our learnings along the way, our new business, *Conscious Business Insights*, and *REAL* Leadership would not be possible. Thank you to Nathan Hassall for his genius in copy-editing. I am deeply grateful to Walter Couture, whose dedication to research throughout the writing and editing process helped bring this book to life. Finally, to all the leaders I've coached and organizations I've worked with: thank you for being such great partners.

Dedication: *To Barry Robertson*
It's been a really amazing journey.
I would not be here without you.

REAL LEADERSHIP: THE TOOLS

The importance of having a strong culture to improve engagement and drive performance is a key asset when trying to improve productivity, speed-to-market, and measurable bottom-line results. Bain & Company sights that, "a culture that inspires and spurs performance make companies 3.7 times more likely to be top performers." At Conscious Business Insights, we believe that conscious, aware, and REAL leaders drive high- performing cultures based on how they behave and lead.

The Conscious Business Insights REAL Leadership assessment is part of our cultural transformation process. We have built a comprehensive and integrated cultural impact and leadership 360 solution. This in-depth protocol was developed based on our proprietary model of cultural leadership. For the past 30 years, working with nearly 35,000 leaders in over 30 countries, our sister company, Stop At Nothing, developed a unique methodology to improve leadership effectiveness and transform cultures. At Stop At Nothing, we focus on customized, unique, face-to-face experiences to help transform individual leadership behaviors, team integration, and cultural change. At Conscious Business Insights, we have developed a unique digitized platform that drives leadership behavior and culture change. We focus on developing REAL leaders, who drive REAL cultures for REAL results.

REAL Leadership: we evaluate leadership behavior for effectiveness and link the results to your corporate culture. The REAL Leadership model focuses on building core leadership capabilities that boost employee engagement and drive results.

Our methodology looks at the underlying behavioral and cultural norms that impact organizational results. We look to discover the root cause of behavioral tendencies of the leaders and teams that drive or inhibit the overall bottom-line results of the company. We assess the collective behavioral impact of the leadership team and assess individual leadership behaviors. Unlike any other leadership tool currently available, the REAL Leadership Assessment™ links leadership behavior, engagement factors, organizational agility, and cultural indicators to bottom-line results.

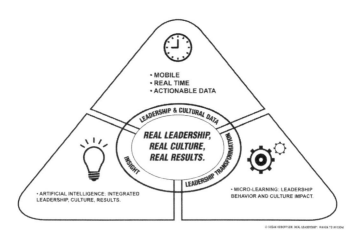

This unique and valuable assessment combines cultural engagement metrics with a leadership 360° report. When executives receive their report, they are able to directly link their leadership behaviors and impact to the cultural environment and how well employees are engaged. Additionally, executives are able to identify specific points of intervention that are required to drive improved performance. The report measures the most impactful leadership skills and capabilities that drive healthy cultures and high-performing teams: **R**esiliency, **E**ngagement, **A**gility, and **L**eading with Wisdom. Our digital technology provides root cause analysis of the behaviors that impede or improve culture.

Next, we help the executive team and individual leaders develop and create key strategic behavioral action plans to improve results. We align leadership behaviors at all levels to support the strategy.

Through digital root cause analysis, we identify the core needs and drivers behind culture and the leadership behaviors that impact the culture. The deep analytics identify who needs to work on what, and automated pushed micro-learning is custom-lined to each individual or team using our system. Individuals and teams are placed on customized learning paths based on real-time measurements.

The outcome is that everyone collectively works on their individual leadership skills, improving the culture that increases employee engagement and drives high-performing organizations. This process gets "everyone" at all levels working on the same common themes. Unlike typical change processes that depend on cross-functional, agile teams, our process is the agile method for high performing cultures and REAL leadership.

Human resource teams benefit because with the heat maps that we provide, they can intervene sooner when an individual or team is not aligning to the cultural values of the organization. Additionally, based on the metrics of the pulsed learning, human resources can make more targeted decisions on what is needed for organizational training and development.

Through our sister company, Stop At Nothing, we provide additional support to organizations by providing the human touch of REAL leadership development and creating REAL cultures. Stop At Nothing (SAN) helps companies make positive changes in their behaviors among individual leaders, teams, and broader organizational cultures. We offer five-day, highly intensive leadership programs along with uniquely customized team sessions.

Our HILS Series (High Impact Leadership Seminar) consists of four 5-day programs. Each program helps leaders develop their REAL leadership skills, improving their emotional intelligence, self-awareness, and self-management while helping leaders develop wisdom. Many of our graduates say this is one of the most positive transformative experiences of their life.

If you would like to attend the HILS program, and you are paying in your own, or you are the first from your company to attend, type in REAL2019 to receive a 20% upon registration. You can register at
www.stopatnothing.com

Our unique methodology for creating high-performing, awareness-based teams and teamwork begins with a deep understanding of the impact the collective leadership team has on organizational performance. Our clients call this process truly transformational.

If you are interested in learning more, please contact:
susan@stopatnothing.com
www.stopatnothing.com
www.cbnsights.com

43596980R00132

Made in the USA
Middletown, DE
26 April 2019